CAREER PLANNING FOR
TEENS

A Fun Guide to Discovering A Successful Path that is Right For You!

Written By: Empower Teens

CONTENTS

🎁 FREE GIFT FOR YOU 📚

As a way of saying thanks for your purchase, we're offering 2 free books for parents and teens!

Get exclusive access to these **FREE** bonuses, go to:

https://empower-teens.com/free-gift

Or scan the QR code right here!

Have any questions? Contact us at info@empower-teens.com

INTRODUCTION

Let's be quite honest: being a teenager can be pretty hard.

Yes, these can be some of the best years of your life. And, yes, you can make some memories that will last you for years. And, yes, you will meet some of the people who will stick with you through thick and thin for decades to come. There are so many rewarding things about being a teenager.

But, at the same time, there are a lot of hurdles, speedbumps, and curve balls that come your way during these special years. And that is just one of the many reasons why being a teen can present a lot of challenges.

You have to deal with your family a lot. You also have to deal with the stress of going to school and getting good grades because, as we all know, you need good grades to pass school and you need to pass school to get far in life. You also have to handle the relationships that are growing in your life, those with friends and even romantic partners.

And you are figuring yourself out too. You are discovering the type of person you are. From your opinions to your feelings to your self-image, it can be a lot to juggle and there is no instruction manual. There is no book given to you when you turn thirteen telling you what to expect and how to handle all of this. You are pretty much thrown into the deep end and have to figure out how to swim.

Yes, it can be a lot.

And perhaps the most pressing and, frankly, frightening part about being a teenager is that you are well aware of what comes after it: adulthood. You are about to set forth on perhaps the most important time period in your life. In just a short few years, you will set out on your own and start to live as a mature, healthy, adult citizen of the world. That requires forethought and planning. It requires that you have a path that you have thought about and chosen and are sticking too.

And discovering that successful path that will lead you into your adult years isn't always easy. But it *is* always necessary.

The good news is that there is a book to help you figure that out: this one.

In the pages that follow, we are going to help you traverse the tricky landscape of moving from your teenage years into your adult ones. We are going to let you look inward, figure out a lot about yourself, explore your possibilities, build a plan, a path, and set forth on it.

The best thing you can do for yourself as an adult is find a career that is rewarding, pays you well, and allows you to live the sort of life that you want to. And in our book, you will find out how to do that. As the end of high school approaches, it is vital that you are planning ahead and figuring out what sort of job you want and, more importantly, how to get and how to enjoy it.

What makes you you? What do you enjoy? What can you imagine pursuing for the rest of your life? What sort of profession will have you waking up every morning with a smile on your face, pep in your step, and a desire to get to work? All of these questions - and so many more - will be asked in the pages ahead.

Let's figure out *your* career path and let's get you stepping forward onto it. Your future is bright, and the time to start crafting it is now!

1 | GET TO KNOW YOURSELF

Before you can figure out the sort of job that will make you happy, you have to answer several questions about yourself.

And, of course, before you can answer these questions about yourself, you have to really and truly know about yourself.

This might sound like a silly thing to say. In fact, it might feel like something you've already done. You see, you live with yourself every single day. In fact, you're the only one who is with you 24/7. You know yourself better than anyone, right? Of course that is true. But there is always room to be more introspective, better acquainted with yourself, and having a better handle on who you are, what you like, what you want, and what you're best at.

And if you really want a career that will not only pay your bills but make you happy at the end of the day, you're going to have to dig deeper and go inward and grasp the sort of person who you are and the dream career that you want.

It'll require some work but, guess what? It's worth it.

Like all hard work, this could be a huge difference-maker and can be key to helping you find the sort of job as an adult that will be rewarding, exciting, and financially sound.

But, how do you wrap your head around...you? How do you figure out more about yourself and determine the career path that will be right for you and only you?

MAKE A LIST AND CHECK IT TWICE

Since you're still in high school, you're well aware of homework assignments. Quite frankly, you're probably tired of them already.

Well, I am sorry to report that I have an assignment for you. But unlike the ones that you get in school, this one is going to give you more than a grade - it's going to give you a path to the career of your dreams. That sounds a little better, doesn't it?

If you want to really know who you are and what drives you and what best suits you in the years ahead, it's time that you make a list. This list will be long, far-reaching, and possibly continually growing. And the subject of the list will be you and only you.

You are going to jost down a list of all the strengths and talents and qualities that you have. This might take a minute, it might go slower than you'd expect.

When you are making this list, think about the ways that other people talk about you. Has anyone ever told you that you're a good listener? Jot it down. Have you been informed that you're a natural leader? Write that down too. Has someone said that you're calm under pressure or always level-headed? Yes, you'll want to write that down too.

All of the personal attributes and qualities that people have spoken about in regards to you need to be written down, no matter how much you believe in them. You might think they are outlandish or way off base but you'll still write them down because if someone else sees them then there is something to that. Remember that sometimes people are able to see things about you that you cannot. Sometimes you need to step outside of yourself to get a good image of how you are. So you need to appreciate and value the things that others say about you.

And of course you need to write down the ways that you see yourself too. Do you feel that you like the clinical and analytical side of math? Write that down. Are you someone who is willing and eager to give a speech and lead a team? You need to write that down too. Do you feel like you handle pressure well and work better when the stakes are high and the heat is on? This is another thing to keep in mind.

As you can see, these are the sorts of attributes that are going to help you figure out the sort of job you want in the near future. If you're not happy being under pressure then you'll likely stay away from positions that are lightning-fast and dealing with an onslaught of customers. If you're more of an analytical person than an outgoing public speaker, this will also come into play when you are weighing the pros and cons of a certain job or career. All of these things are going to add up and they are going to help you figure out the sort of dream job that will keep you excited, well-paid, and, really, in your element.

THE GOOD & THE BAD

While you are going to be writing down many positives about you, it's also very important that you're honest with yourself and you write down some of your shortcomings too when you are getting to know yourself with this list.

Let's be quite frank: all of us have some pitfalls and disadvantages when it comes to work. Some people, for instance, just can't seem to get a great handle on math and science. Others are really lacking when it comes to mastering computers.

At the same time, others are not always great at being social and working in tandem with teams. And some other people hate working by themselves and only get into mental trouble when they aren't working with others. Some people are easily distracted and some people aren't natural leaders but terrific team members instead.

Some of these attributes might sound like you're putting yourself down or being too hard on yourself but you're really just being honest. And that is very important because you need to be sincere and authentic when you talk about the things you can and can't do and the things you like and dislike.

If you want a job that you'll love, you need to know what attracts you and what doesn't, what you're good at and what you're bad at.

THE LIST CONTINUES

Now, just because this list is over doesn't mean you're done making them. There is another list you have to make and this one is going to be a bit more fun and exciting.

This list is going to be one that consists of all the areas of interest in your life. You can go big here and not really hold back. There is no wrong answer on this list.

Do you love writing? Do you like being artistic and creative? Or do you like making plans, writing outlines, and then implementing them? Are you a fan of music or the performing arts? Do you like painting? Are you someone who loves coffee, wine, or high-end food? Make sure you write all of this down.

By doing so, you are coloring a picture of yourself and filling out your personality and figuring out the sort of things that really drive you, make you happy, and inspire you.

Some people feel like this part of the process is silly because they feel like there is no way they'll ever be creative for a living or writing for a full-time job. These feel like pie-in-the-sky qualities about them that won't ever have an impact on the sort of profession they have.

But this is a vital part of the process because it is going to help you really get in touch with the things that really fire you up. Sure, you might not be writing novels like JK Rowling or Stephen King but that doesn't mean you can't find a job where writing, even creatively, is part of your duties and role. Jobs like that *do* exist out there and most of them have room for upward mobility and climbing the ladder and achieving more once you prove yourself.

The point of this part of the process is to figure out the things that make you happy. In the near future, we are going to remember that when you are weighing possible career paths for you.

Make your list, check it twice, sit on it for a few days, and then add to it if it feels right. Remember, there is no correct length or method to do this. You are simply writing down features about yourself and painting a fuller, more helpful image of yourself so you can use it going forward and pursue the sort of job that will really make you happy.

CAREER TESTS?

There may have been a point during your high school career when you sat down and took a career assessment test. What are these and how do they work? They will have you answer many questions to figure out the type of employee you can be and the sort of career that you'd be best at. They will ask you about problem solving and how you work with others and the sort of mental roadblocks that get in your way the most.

These types of tests have been used for generations with a varying degree of success. Sadly, some of them are now very outdated and they don't work as well as people say. And sometimes people feel defeated when they are given an assessment that they don't like. How would you feel being told you'd be a great corporate lawyer when you have never even considered that before? Not great, I bet. That is one of the risks you run when you are doing these sorts of career tests.

But there is good news when it comes to career assessments. That is that there are now plenty of them online that you can take, completely for free. You don't have to go to your high school counselor to take one anymore.

Now, it's important to remember this: these tests are not an exact science. They are not going to be 100% accurate and some of them are going to be completely off-based online. But the thing that they will provide you with is ideas. Maybe some of these tests will come back to you with jobs that you have never considered and immediately sound promising to you. Sometimes these tests think of things that haven't crossed your mind.

Here is the best news of all: we have compiled some special career tests that could help you get on the path you want. We have a bunch of bonus content filled with assessments. And we have gone to great lengths to make sure we are offering you only the very best of the best. So make sure that you scan the QR and run through the tests that we have provided. This will be a great way to set yourself up for greatness and find the career that is waiting for you.

CONCLUSION

Instead of thinking of these career tests - whether official or from the web - as definitive and absolute, think of them as a way to generate ideas and brainstorm potential careers that you haven't had on your radar. You never know, one of these tests might present you with a potential path that sounds like it's tailor-made for you.

You can reach out to your counselor and ask about a career test. They will definitely be able to point you in the right direction and will likely give you access to some of the more trusted and most proven assessments out there.

Or you can just hop online today and search for career tests. Take a few of them and see what the results are. Do they give you a common consensus? Are they all wildly different? Pore over the results and see if an imagine of your possible career is coming to light.

2 | EXPLORE THE POSSIBILITIES

So we have already figured out a bit more about you and the sort of worker you would be. We know what motivates you, what bores you, what fires you up and what leaves you deflated and not interested.

But just because you know the sort of employee you can be and the sort of job responsibilities that you'd like, you don't know all of the professions out there waiting for you. But the good news is that you can find out about all of the careers that are possible.

Now more than ever before, there are plenty of ways to find out about particular career paths and potential jobs that could pay your bills and make you happy to work daily.

WHAT IS A CAREER CLUSTER?

I don't blame you if you've never heard of a career cluster before. It sounds like something almost alien and bizarre.

But studying these clusters and imagining yourself working with them is a great way to better understand what job might be right for you.

The National Career Clusters Framework is a well-researched, com-plicated, and time-tested tool that is used by CTE, or the Career

Technical Education. Within the National Career Clusters Framework are 16 career clusters.

What this is is basically a way to look at the broad groups of jobs and industries created by the US Department of Education. It can help you and many others create a career path that is right for you. States all over the country have adopted all 16 of these career clusters. If you're looking for the right job for you, this is a great way to start finding it.

Here is what you should do with these career clusters. You should look at each of them, do some research, and think about yourself pursuing each of them. So, without further ado, let's list all of the career clusters that are out there and decide how they can help you.

- Agriculture, Food & Natural Resources
- Architecture & Construction
- Arts, Audio/Video Technology & Communications
- Business, Management & Administration
- Education & Training
- Finance
- Government & Public Administration
- Health Science
- Hospitality & Tourism
- Human Services
- Information Technology
- Law, Public Safety, Corrections & Security
- Manufacturing
- Marketing, Sales & Service
- Science, Technology, Engineering & Mathematics
- Transportation, Distribution & Logistics

Obviously some of these industries might not feel enticing to you. Maybe you have zero interest in working for the government or pursuing a job revolving around audio and visual arts.

But maybe one or more of those clusters have caught your eye. Does the concept of working in hospitality and tourism sound good to you? Maybe marketing is something that you could be good at. How do you feel when you think of being a sales person or dealing with logistics?

See, the career clusters that people have used for years can help you too. Now, they might not give you the exact job that you could thrive at but they might better help you craft a path and give you a clearer image of the sort of industry that you might do great at. At this point in our process, we are simply trying to figure out the type of worker you would be and the type of industries that could be beneficial and rewarding - both mentally and financially - to you.

At this point in finding out what sort of career is right for you, the point of the career clusters is to just set you up in the right direction and perhaps open your eyes and your mind to the sort of work that you can do in the future.

Why is this so important? Why should you care at all about career clusters? Well, for a number of reasons. Firstly, maybe you don't have any vague idea of what sort of job you want in your life. Maybe you don't even have the faintest clue of what feels right to you. If that's the case, the career clusters can really expose you to a whole bunch of jobs that you may have not known of. Maybe you have been totally and completely clueless so far when it comes to figuring out what comes next for you once you enter adulthood. There is nothing wrong with that! But if that's your situation, the career clusters can really help.

Another reason why career clusters can be such a helpful tool is because they can inform you of the sort of training and education that you might need if you want to take the steps forward and move ahead pursuing one of those fields. Some of these types of jobs have very specific requirements that you will need to meet if you want them. You will have to do certain schooling, get certifications, and pass tests. It could require a lot of studying. And, of course, that also requires time. Therefore, looking into these career clusters is smart because it will allow you the time and planning needed to make sure you are qualified to achieve them in the future.

Or maybe you had some sort of idea but you weren't entirely sure. Maybe you had an inkling that you want to work in hospitality or media but you're not sure what sort of job within that field you want. These career clusters will be the first step to finding that job of your dream. It starts by just investigating the career clusters but is followed up with a deeper dive. And that is what comes next. You have seen the career clusters and the vague, somewhat ambiguous fields that they cover. Now it is time for you to look into the specific jobs within them.

EXPLORE SPECIFIC CAREERS

If you have looked through the career clusters that we spoke about and one or a few of them speak to you, call out to you, appeal to you, you're in luck. That is a positive and important first step to finding out the career of your dreams.

However, it is now time for you to do some hard work and dig a bit deeper into the career clusters that appealed to you. You need to really peel back each of these clusters and find out which jobs within them make the most sense to you.

For example, let's say that you were really taken by an energy career cluster. On the surface, you might not be sure what that all entails. What sort of jobs are associated with energy? Quite a few. For example, you may work for an energy company, you may be a technician, you may be someone who installs and manages power lines and fixes them when a storm comes to town, whether out in the streets or back at headquarters. Those are just some of the many careers that are buried deep within the energy career cluster.

As you can see, you now have a lot more options that are much more specific. And within that, you will have more choices now. Not all of the jobs within an entire industry are going to appeal to you. Some are going to sound too draining or too intensive when it comes to working with others. Maybe some of the jobs require a lot of teamwork and you feel like you're a bit more of a lone wolf, who works best when he or she is alone. There are plenty of reasons why some jobs will look good for you, and some others will not.

Another career cluster that is packed full of multiple different types of jobs is the one of education and training. We have all had teachers in our lives who have impacted us and made us feel so much better about ourselves, our potential, and the path that we are on. We know just how powerful and life-changing that can be. Could you be the sort of teacher for someone? Could you be the type that will touch the lives of your student?

Well, the good news is that even if you don't think that's your lot in your life, there are plenty of other professions within the education and training cluster that could be right for you. Maybe you're an office assistant at the front office of a school, maybe you work in admissions, maybe you're a school counselor, or perhaps a maintenance worker. There are just so many education jobs that exist out there. The same is true for training. Training involves teaching people who might not necessarily be students. Think about employees at a business, who need to be trained in a variety of things, from customer service to technical work, and beyond. All of that training needs to be handled by a professional who knows what they are doing.

The key at this point is to look into any of the career clusters that sound good to you and see what they have to offer. Dig deep, look at all the options, see which one feels and looks right to you, and start working hard to pursue the job that you like most. Also, don't just write off a career path because you are not completely riveted by the way a career cluster comes across to you. Just because you're not blown away by how a career cluster is direscribe doesn't mean it might be wrong for you. You need to dig a bit deeper, look a bit more, and see what it all has to offer. You never know what is waiting for you within each of these career clusters. But you'll only find out if you do the hard, but important work of looking into each and every one of them.

EXPLORE THE JOB MARKET

Now, just because you might have a better idea of what you want with your career doesn't mean it's necessarily going to be an easy path to it. The truth of the matter is that even in the best of times, it might be hard to find the sort of job that you want. But that is even more true when the economy isn't 100% strong or the market that you're trying to break into is flush with potential employees.

In short, there may be some challenges waiting for you when it comes to landing your dream job. That surely complicates the entire process. Does it make it impossible? Absolutely not, but it definitely will throw a monkey wrench into your plans at times.

The best way to overcome these problems and have a better understanding of what the current job market is like is to study it. You need to understand what current employers are looking for, expecting, and how they are hiring.

This means that if you have found a job or a career cluster that feels right for you, it's now your responsibility to do the work needed to make yourself a wonderful candidate for it. Remember earlier when we mentioned some of the training or classes or certifications you might need to land particular jobs? Now is the time for you to take the bull by the horns and make sure you have passed them all, done everything that is needed, and have positioned yourself to be hired.

Also, you should be doing some studying of the jobs that most appeal to you. You need to do this for a couple of reasons. Firstly, and most importantly, you need to know all the things that are waiting for you if you ever end up landing that job. You need to know the job requirements, what the actual profession is like and what it calls for day in and day out. But you also need to know some of the challenges, some of the things that will perhaps slow you down or make your work harder. No job is filled with nothing but great times and wonderful days. They are all going to have their drawbacks and bad days and you need to know what is causing them. You need to know the good, the bad, and the ugly about all jobs.

But another reason why you should be studying any profession that you could possibly pursue is because you need to know how to set yourself up for success when it comes to applying for the job. You should be familiar with what the job is calling for and what the companies within the industry expect. This will better prepare you for the process of actually getting the job. If you know what is expected of you and what you will be asked and what you need to be an expert at, you will be ready to go when the time comes and you are sitting down face-to-face with a potential employee.

Think of it this way: you need to be an expert about the job that you are looking to land. You should know more than just what it pays and a vague idea of the sort of responsibilities that you'll have. Instead, you need to study the profession and know it well, inside and out. Then and only then will you have what it takes to set yourself up to actually land the job. An employer will jump at the chance of hiring you if you make it clear that not only you have what it takes but you are also an expert in everything that could come with the job, both good and bad.

ATTEND RESEARCH FAIRS

One of the best ways to get a really good handle of a new job that might be right for you is to attend a job fair and ask around.

Job fairs are held throughout the country, and you can find them advertised all over the place, specifically on the social media accounts of your local city government.

What is a job fair and how can it help you? A job fair is pretty much exactly what it sounds like. With a job fair, you will see a whole bunch of employers, in person, who are seeking new talent for their businesses. Why is this so important?

For a number of reasons. The biggest reason why you want to do this is because it will help you leave a lasting impression on the person who matters most: your prospective employer. Imagine just how great it would be for you and your chances of landing a job if you are able to make the boss smile, laugh, and feel good about you? They would walk away from the experience feeling good about the whole thing. Then when you eventually come to them looking for a job, they will remember your bright face, the questions that you asked, and the overall great personality that you presented. Clearly, this will help get your foot in the door and will go a long way to making sure you get the job.

But another great thing about a job fair is that it serves as a sort of research experiment, a way to get intel. You should be asking questions of the people at the job fairs. You should be picking their brains, dissecting their positions, and getting a much better understanding of what the job entails and all that it brings.

It is vital that you don't just ask the easy questions too. Don't just ask them what their favorite part of their profession is. Instead, inquire about the hardest parts of the job, the training that is needed, the education you will also need, the pay that you will receive. Don't be afraid to ask questions that go below just the surface level. Some people are too timid to do this but it can't hurt you. In fact, it will show that you're much more serious and aggressive about getting the job and doing it perfectly.

Another great way to leave an impact at these job fairs is to ask each and every professional there about upward mobility and the chance for growth within the company. People who ask these sorts of questions are people who are looking to do a great job, go above and beyond, earn their keep, and only get better and more important to the company. They are the ones who often climb the ladder. They start as a bottom rung employee and, within time, are the ones who someday lead the business as a manager or beyond.

When you are done with a job fair, you should take home a bunch of literature that is given out by the companies that are present. They will offer you tons of fliers and sheets and business cards and you should keep them all and make sure you take special note of the ones that had the most appeal to you. When the time comes, you will reach out to the people who gave you their business cards and you will make sure they remember you from the job fair.

Speaking of, it's not a bad idea to have business cards of your own at this point in the process. You obviously won't have a specific profession to list on the card, but you can still put your name, phone number, maybe a short blurb about you, and other contact information. Any way that you can appeal and leave an impact on the people running the job fair will go a long way to making sure that you are the first person they want to talk to when they are hiring.

MAKE A LIST

Are you ready to make another list? You better be because this part of the job-hunting process is to narrow down everything you have taken into account and all the things you have learned and focus even closer on the sort of jobs that are going to be right for you.

You have gone through all the career clusters. You have also taken a more specialized and deeper look at the actual jobs within them. And you have even gone to job fairs and rubbed elbows and had chats with the people who are in power and can provide you with the career you wanted.

Now it's time to trim some of the fat.

After doing so much research and meeting so many people, you should start to cross off the jobs that you don't think are going to be right for you. It is time to exercise some of the professions that first caught your eye.

Why should you do that? Shouldn't you leave yourself with plenty of options? While that sounds like a good idea on the surface - and it is in many ways - it is important that you don't have too many options as you start to hunt for the career of your dreams. That is because you need to start to find more focus and limit your options and, therefore, limit the number of places you are applying to and the amount of effort you are putting into your hunt for a job. If you are looking into too many places at one time then you are going to be spreading yourself thin. You will be looking in so many places that you won't be focused and you won't be able to actually zero in on just one job that you can pursue. And, of course, in the end, you only want one job.

So you should take the list of possible professions that you made and start to cross off the ones that aren't right for you. Maybe it's because they don't pay enough. Maybe it's because their hours aren't great. Maybe it's because you didn't get a good feel from the employers in that industry when you were at the job fair. From pay rate to educational requirements to location to just about any other reason, there will be things that pop up that make it clear that maybe you should move past certain jobs and instead focus on others. This is good, this is great. This will help you narrow down your search and move forward. By narrowing down the search, you are going to give yourself a better chance at getting a job. You can put more attention and energy into being the best employee for one type of job instead of being a really good one for several.

It is time for you to start to cross off jobs that aren't going to work and turn your attention, deeply, to others. By doing so, you are going to be setting yourself up for a clear path to success.

CONCLUSION

Possibilities - there sure are a lot of them, aren't there? This chapter has shown you that you will have quite a few choices to select from when you are hunting for the job of your dreams.

In fact, there are so many choices that might be right for you that it can feel downright overwhelming. That is why we have given you choices and tips that you should keep in mind in the weeks and months and years ahead.

First and foremost, you need to again be very honest with yourself. You need to look inside yourself and determine what sort of employee you are and what type of job you want to pursue. This is vital because it will not only ensure that you have the sort of job that is right for you but you will also be sure that you don't ever get tired of your profession or find out you made the wrong choice years down the line.

Honesty is crucial because only you know what is right for you and what you really want out of your career. And you will only know this if you ask good, hard, deep questions and really examine the sort of worker you are and the sort of job that you can tackle.

Career clusters are important too and too many people write them off or don't know about them at all. Use them as a tool to really un-derstand the many number of industries that exist out there. Once you have seen a few career clusters that catch your eye, you should do a deeper dive and look into the sort of education and training you might need as well as the job responsibilities that come with each and every job within the cluster.

You owe it to yourself to respectfully and honestly look at yourself and the job market that exists and all the professions within it. This is the only way to make sure that you are setting yourself up for success and a long, exciting career in any given field that you choose.

3 | FILTER DOWN OPTIONS

Let's be honest: you want to find a career in an industry that is going to have space for you. You want to locate and succeed in a job that has a chance for growth, more pay, more potential,

But that isn't always possible.

You happen to be growing up in a time when the job market is very... bizarre, to put it gently. There are a number of contributing factors to this. But the bottom line is this: it might not be as easy for you to get a job as it was for your parents and their parents before them. You might face more challenges and you might have different options and you might have to do things that they simply did not. You might be rewarded better, of course. Many of the jobs that your parents once had probably didn't come with the high rate of pay and the benefits that you may acquire, for instance.

But it is important that you are honest and realize the job market that you are entering is different from the ones that came before. And it brings a slew of challenges - and benefits.

How do you make it through all of this? How do you avoid the land-mines, escape the traps, and find the sort of job that is right for you? You do this by filtering through the junk jobs and the dead-end leads and the things that aren't promising at all. Filtering is key when you are first entering the job market as a young adult and it's the best way for you to push through all the noise, avoid the jobs that won't lead anywhere, and wasting your time.

IDENTITY IN—DEMAND CAREERS

What are some of the top jobs this year that can pay you the best and also provide you with a career that you'd love to have for years until retirement? That is a loaded and tricky question - but it does have an answer.

Now, there is an important difference to highlight here. You need to know how to determine what is an in-demand job and what is a job that has many in-demand positions.

What's the difference? It's quite a big one. An in-demand job is one that many people are trying to apply for and fill. And an in-demand position is one that employers are eager to hire for. Obviously, you have better luck at landing an in-demand position but you might get paid better and enjoy yourself more with an in-demand position. That's because those positions are in-demand for a reason, right? Whether it be the benefits they provide, the pay they give, or the sort of work they ask, these are the jobs that many people want.

So, what are some of the most in-demands that are out there right now?

You will find that any career related to software development is going to be in-demand for a number of reasons. First and foremost, it pays very well. And it's vitally important too.

The pay for software developers has increased over the years more and more as these jobs have become more pivotal and crucial for a number of businesses. Now you can make a very comfortable living if you are pursuing a career in software development. These are the people who do all sorts of incredibly important things. They make the programs and the apps that not only customers use, but companies too.

From creating POS systems to websites, inventory programs, and more, the entire world functions because software allows us to.

Some things to keep in mind with this sort of job. Firstly, you will be competing against the best of the best. Your generation is one that is very comfortable and talented when it comes to computers and software. That wasn't the case just a few years ago. Yours is the first generation that grew up with iPhones, iPads, and easy access to mastering this sort of work. While that means you are much more talented in this field, it also means that your peers are too.

And, because of that, your peers will become your competitors too.

This means that you will want to make sure you really know this type of work before you pursue a job in this field. Just having basic knowledge of it isn't going to be good enough, especially when you are competing against other people who are just as driven as you are.

Luckily for you, there are plenty of ways for you to hone your skills and get even better with software development. You can take extra courses online, at your local community college, and on various websites too. There is no shortage of information out there that will provide you with more skill and help you get even better at software development. Spend time looking up YouTube videos and practicing at home if this is something that excites you. Position yourself to be the best of the best before you even apply for the job.

There are more high-paying in-demand jobs that could appeal to you. Yes, many of them are related to tech. Project managers, data analysts, and engineers are just a few of the computer-savvy jobs that could help you live a comfortable life with a good salary.

But there are more old-fashioned and reliable jobs that are still in-demand too. For example, the world always needs plenty of nurses.

Indeed, a registered nurse is one of the most sought-after jobs and has been for generations too.

Now, being a nurse is perhaps one of the most challenging careers that exists. Not only are the hours long and draining, but you are subjected to very stressful situations. Indeed, you are often confronted with life-or-death choices when it comes to being a nurse. And most people who start their careers as nurses finish them as one too. This isn't the sort of job that you only pick up for a summer and then move on from. If you are thinking of being a nurse, you should be prepared to be one for years, even decades.

Within the medical field, you will find plenty of other jobs that are always needing new blood. Medical technologists, physician assistants, and physical therapists are just some of them. All of them are high-paying and highly rewarding in their own ways.

What do all of these jobs have in common? As you can guess, they require intensive, hands-on training that you will have to spend a lot of time on. They are not the sorts of jobs that you can just walk into and start without some classes, months and months of them in fact. Again, these are careers, not side hustles or summer jobs that you will pick up and then leave behind shortly thereafter.

WHAT'S NEXT ON THE JOB MARKET?

A young, driven worker like you should be thinking ahead if you really want to find the next sort of job that will provide you with a heft paycheck, comfortable living, and enjoyable career.

Did you know that between now and 2027, more than 69 million jobs will be created worldwide. That's an awful lot of jobs, isn't it? But hold on, there is a catch: in that same time period, the market will also eliminate more than 83 million positions, mostly due to the advancement of technology, such as AI.

The rise of AI and other tech solutions can make life easier for many companies but it can also make it harder for people like you to find a job that you can rely on and enjoy for years. That means that you have to be proactive and think ahead and find out what is going to be the sort of job that you can have, through thick and thin, good and bad, no matter what sort of impact AI has on the global economy.

Recently, the job-finding site Indeed created a list of professions that will have the most promise in the years ahead, as the world changes drastically and technology makes itself more known in the sort of jobs we have taken for granted for generations. What are some of the professions that will still have a lot of promise through 2027 and beyond?

HOME HEALTH AIDE

A home health aide is someone who comes to a client's house and takes care of them one-on-one, in-person, several days a week. Their roles include dressing and personal hygiene, making sure clients take their medications, and also communicating and working with medical professionals to keep tabs on a client's overall health standards.

As you can imagine, this job is always important and always will be but it comes with its own set of challenges. You have to have medical training, for one, even though you won't be carrying out tasks as complicated as what a doctor does. Secondly, you can face some emotional stressors during this job and can experience some emotionally intensive, even traumatic moments. Of course, you also have to adjust to the personality and quirks of the person you are working for.

Some of the patients who need home health aides aren't the easiest to deal with. Are you up for that? If you are, you could be looking at a job that comes with plenty of rewards and a chance at wonderful memories too. No formal education is needed beyond the certification from National Association for Home Care & Hospice.

CONSTRUCTION WORKER

No matter what is going on in the world, construction workers will always be needed. Buildings will always be built and trained professionals will forever be the ones who do this. Even in the worst time when construction projects slow, this is still a job that can be mostly reliable and also mostly beneficial when it comes to a paycheck.

The responsibilities in this job are pretty much what you'd imagine. Construction workers rake up debris from job sites, assemble framework for buildings, run equipment that transports building supplies, and help any specialized craft workers with their tasks. It's hard work and you should be prepared for long hours in sometimes unpleasant conditions. Since you will be spending a lot of time outside, be ready to get dirty and sweaty. But you could be rewarded handsomely with a strong salary that could be upwards of $40,000 a year. Plus, at your young age, you have the sort of energy that lends itself well to an employee in the construction industry.

Additionally, this is one of the few jobs that you *can* leave behind after a year or two. There are in fact some students who work in construction while they are studying at college. The pay is good, the experience is tiring but rewarding, and you can walk away with a pretty penny after a short amount of time.

Be aware that certain jobs in this industry may need you to have prior experience obtained through an apprenticeship or trade school. That isn't true across the board and it depends on the company that you are working for. Construction jobs can also be found simply by knowing someone in the industry already who is willing to vouch for you.

DATA SCIENCE

Being a student yourself, you know just how important analyzing data is and you have done so many times during your time in school. What if you heard that studying and using data for businesses of all types was one of the most promising jobs for the next decade and beyond?

Becoming a data scientist might be one of the smartest moves you can make if you are thinking of the long term. Data evaluation and application are the responsibility of data scientists. With careful training and analysis, these professionals foresee events and trends for insurance and financial corporations, academic institutions, research organizations, and healthcare services, among others by using their broad understanding of mathematics, forecasting, and statistical interpretations. To achieve this, data scientists design experiments, surveys, and polls and use mathematical and statistical methods to anticipate outcomes and determine the root causes of problems.

The thing that is so promising about data science is that many companies are catching on to how helpful it is and are starting to use it too. That bodes well for you if this is a career you want to try. The data science industry is anticipated to expand significantly over the next few years as businesses of all sizes and types depend on data analysts to supply the information that underpins crucial business decisions.

During the years to come, a significant portion of economic development is projected to be supported by the expanded use of data analysis for making educated decisions about business, health care, and policy. Now that so many successful companies know just how helpful data science can be, there is every reason to believe it'll keep growing in the next decade and beyond.

TEACHERS

Although there is already a lot of demand for this position, it is very possible that this will grow in the future. No matter how advanced artificial intelligence becomes, there is no doubt that teachers will always be needed.

Yes, it is anticipated that the function of teaching may incorporate greater use of technology in the future, but it is still anticipated that a human person will still be required to conduct lessons to the children of the world.

Even if technology takes great leaps and bounds, future teachers will still be required to plan classes, grade papers, as well as provide assistance for students because these are the present jobs that technology hasn't been able to fully automate. And as good as a computer becomes, nothing will beat the one-on-one conversation and connection that only a human teacher can give a young student.

Online education has gained increasing attention over the last few years due to the COVID pandemic, altering how lessons are taught. Less tangible paperwork, including online assignments and classrooms, equals less clutter in instructors' homes, classrooms, and luggage. But even with that, the importance of human teachers has become very clear and that ensures that educators will always be required.

It is important to note that many teachers don't get paid what they deserve. Depending on the part of the country they work in, they could even need a second job to make ends meet. There are indeed many challenges that come with teaching but many rewards too. Think of that teacher who touched your heart and changed your life when you were young - you had just as important an impact on them as they did on you. That's very rewarding, as you can imagine.

HOSPITALITY

As you remember, there were several years recently when people weren't able to meet up with one another and enjoy company like they were used to. That was quite a challenge, wasn't it? And it showed just how important one-on-one interaction and the industry of hospitality was. Now that the virus is thankfully behind us, jobs related to hospitality, catering, and other related industries are all the more important.

There are many different types of jobs within the hospitality industry. Some of them relate to throwing a party. Are you looking to have good food and drink with an event that you are having? A hospitality company can help with that. Or maybe you're staying at a hotel and you want great service at the front desk checking you in. Again, that is hospitality.

Hospitality jobs have been crucial for both employers and employees for generations now and that should still be the case in the decades to come. The need for hospitality and catering personnel will actually likely increase in the future. From waiters and waitresses to chefs to bar staff to hotel and motel workers, brushing up on these abilities will undoubtedly help you find a career in the future.

PROPERTY DEVELOPMENT

Locations to reside and work are necessities for everyone in the globe. Careers in real estate, building, and architecture may all be found in property development. Although there is a need for realtors world-wide, some areas may be more suited for potential realtors because of the larger demand and higher average compensation. To obtain their license, real estate agents must pass a real estate exam.

Jobs in real estate development are ideal for those with strong problem-solving skills, a desire to build livable communities for individuals and families, and a preference for manual labor in the case of building. If you want to work in the real estate industry, developing strong economic, sustainable design, and building practices knowledge is a must.

ARTS

The term "arts and humanities" may be used to describe a wide range of fine and applied arts as well as professions that derive from a number of related disciplines of study. Careers in dancing, painting, music, writing, filmmaking, and other fine and applied arts are available.

Although these artistic jobs are not recognized for being profitable, people who pursue them might find them to be engaging and gratifying. Filmmakers are an exception to this rule, as many of them have highly lucrative positions in their industry. In contrast to visual artists who are expected to have little to no employment growth, film workers are expected to see substantial job growth.

A significant approach to give back to your town and to the human experience as a whole is to become an artist. Most people would agree that engaging with and appreciating art in some way improves their lives. Artists must be perceptive, sensitive to the nuances of the human condition, and willing to work hard to develop their skills. They must be able to express themselves in a unique way that adds something fresh to the aesthetic environment of their culture or group.

Humanities-related jobs call for a variety of abilities. Those who are self-motivated and enthusiastic about their surroundings might choose these careers. They frequently call for the capacity to pick things up on the job and adjust to novel situations. These vocations can benefit from critical thinking skills, the capacity for problem-solving creativity, as well as the capacity for team leadership and public speaking.

LEGAL

One of the professional paths that requires the most schooling is becoming a lawyer. Before obtaining a law degree and clearing the bar test, lawyers first need to get an undergraduate degree. Although the lengthy process, being a lawyer may lead to a fulfilling profession. First, a lot of attorneys make a lot of money. Public clients can also receive crucial legal assistance from attorneys. If you wish to practice law, you can also be enthusiastic about specializing in a certain area of the law, such as immigration, domestic, or criminal law.

Excellent writing and public speaking abilities are prerequisites for working as a lawyer. Attorneys must have a thorough understanding of the law and be able to develop compelling arguments to support their clients' causes.

CODING

One of the most in-demand talents for technology organizations is quickly evolving to be coding.

Some European nations have begun incorporating coding into their basic school curricula in response to the growing relevance of programming.

Without a doubt, coding will open up new career opportunities in the future. Yet, there is an evident vacuum that has to be filled for the instant coding market because it can be quite a while for those elementary school students to reach the employment market.

Hence, if you want to take advantage of a chance, now could be the finest moment to start a software development business ever.

You can do anything you like with programming since there are so many separate things you can accomplish using it. Perhaps creating video games appeals to you, or maybe writing code for software is more your style. Or maybe you like creating programs for companies and the way that they do inventory and sell products. The possibilities are pretty much endless when you get into coding.

CONTENT CREATOR

During the past several years, there has been an enormous and in-disputable surge in content producers. So what exactly is a content producer? This is a rather all-encompassing phrase that includes anybody who produces media for digital platforms. Yet, social media influencers are the category of content creators with the most renown.

The need for content makers is expected to increase in the coming years as more material is consumed everyday than ever before.

The opportunities for this job path are also pretty much limitless, from food bloggers to vloggers. Of course, it's not just as easy as creating a blog and then immediately finding success. Instead, you will have to really understand the market. In other words, you will have to understand the viewers and readers that you are trying to woo. After that, you will have to get really good at your job and make sure that you are continually creating content that will bring people back again and again. There is a lot of hard work and energy that is put into being a successful content creator. It's not nearly as easy as it appears!

DATA PROTECTION

The number of regulations governing data processing and privacy is increasing. You have seen the countless headlines related to data protection and the ways that online thieves are stealing everything from social security numbers to bank account information. Billions, if not trillions, of dollars have been lost due to data being stolen.

Our date is very important and we trust the companies that we give it to, such as our banks and our schools and even the companies that write our paychecks. Sadly, all too frequently, our data is mishandled or unlawfully used after getting into the wrong hands. This will lead to the creation of new positions for data detectives, who are responsible for upholding data regulations, to track out how specific corporations are using data.

Several enterprises, political parties, educational institutions, and other organizations are already hiring thousands of people for data protection-related positions since these investigations have already begun. And over the next decade and beyond, more and more of these jobs will pop up. It truly can be one of the most beneficial and popular professions of the future.

To get into data protection, training will be necessary. You'll obviously have to know your way around a computer, data centers, servers, and more. And you'll also have to be able to communicate well too because many data protection professionals have to report back to the companies they are hired by. They have to write reports, create and implement changes, and communicate problems and how they have been and can be solved.

ENTREPRENEUR

Remember that today's culture is more enterprising than ever before. The typical individual today has a greater opportunity to create an individual business or a tiny empire because of the internet and technical improvements. These options to launch your own firm will only increase as more technological milestones are reached.

There hasn't been a better moment to become an entrepreneur and provide your concept a shot to flourish if you have a company idea or desire. But with so many opportunities come so many challenges too. You have to compete against a market full of people who also believe wholly in their ideas and think they have what it takes to break through the noise and competition and create a company that has a long, lasting effect.

What makes your idea different? What makes it better? Why would others want to buy into it, invest in it, and use it? Being an entrepreneur isn't solely about coming up with an idea that you think can make you some money. It is about building upon that idea, investing your energy into it, and crafting it, evolving it, and perfecting it.

The good news is that you are young, which means that you have your finger on the pulse of the most important demographic. Companies always take off when they are able to appeal to and sell themselves to young people. Since you are still tuned into what your generation wants and needs, you will be able to capitalize on that and build upon and make money because of it. This can be your key to taking your idea and transforming it into something special, and financially successful too.

HOW TO FILTER DOWN YOUR OPTIONS

You will not be able to catch good and juicy fish with too big of a net. And the same is relatively true when you are looking for a job or career for your future. You will not be able to find a job that can be rewarding for your long term unless you do the work to narrow your search and make sure you are looking in the right ways.

With your immense amount of talent as well as youth, you have a surplus of jobs that could be perfect for you. That is why you need to take the extra step of making sure you are limiting the jobs you are looking at. If you don't do the filtering needed, you'll be forever looking but never employed.

Okay, so how do you do that? How do you filter and narrow down all of your options and stay strictly focused on what is really right for you?

WHY ARE YOU DOING IT?

This is a question that you should ask often when you are trying to find a career: why are you doing what you're doing? Why are you taking this job? Why are you pursuing this position? Is it because of the money or something deeper? Is there something about this job that feels emotionally and mentally rewarding? Something that goes beyond just a nice, comfy paycheck?

See how we said you should ask this when you're looking for a career? That is because there is a large difference between a job and a career. Generally, a job is a way to make ends meet and make sure you can pay your bills and keep a roof above your head. A career, on the other hand, is something that can give you all of that but also keep you happy and satisfied for years and decades to come.

This book is about helping you find and plan for a career, not just a job that you will keep for a short time. We are not about helping you find a gig. Instead, we are about helping you find a career that you might be passionate about for the rest of your life.

So, ask yourself: why? And ask yourself what too. What makes you happy? Why do you want this profession? We have mentioned before, but you have to dig deep to really get the sort of answer that is going to help you.

If you can't easily answer either of those questions about a job, it's a pretty good indicator that it might not be right for you, at least not for the long term future. If you're solely following a job for the money that it pays, that isn't the sort that will give you a career you can rely on and build a life around.

Here is another big, important question you should ask when you are narrowing down your job search: can you imagine doing this when you are ten, twenty, even thirty years older? If the answer to that is no, that's okay. But it definitely means that this isn't a career for you. Instead, it's a job.

CAN THIS HELP YOU ACHIEVE LONG-TERM GOALS?

If you're narrowing down all your options on the hunt for a life-long career then you need to think of the goals you have. And not just the goals you have for now (pay off your car, get rid of student loan debt) but also the ones that you'll have in the future (buy a house, raise a family, travel extensively).

Does the job you're looking into allow you to reach all of those goals? Your career should not be the only important part of your life but it should help you achieve a lot. It might be fun and it could involve some people you greatly value but does your current job allow you to build the sort of life that you have always envisioned? If not, it might not be the career for you but rather a job that you hold for now as you search for your life-long position.

GET ADVICE FROM OTHERS

One of the best ways for you to narrow down the amount of jobs presented before you at your young age is to look to the people who have pursued them all and see how happy and successful they are.

We have all worked jobs with "old timers" who have been there for ages. They have made their jobs into careers. Are they happy? Do they seem satisfied? Do they constantly praise the job they have or complain about it? Is that the sort of person you think you'd be if you followed this career path for the rest of your life?

Now, you might not be comfortable enough to come straight out and ask people how they feel about their jobs but you can often get a feel for how satisfied they are with their positions and the years they've poured into it.

Having a career is a commitment and it lasts for years. Sometimes that is very rewarding for people and sometimes it kind of sucks their souls away. You need to do a careful consideration of the impact that a career might have on your well-being. Looking to the people who have already followed it is a great way to do this. Look at them, think of yourself and your future, and determine if this is really a path you want to follow. If not, it is time to move on!

CONCLUSION

Finding the right career for you is about analyzing. It's about taking a look at the data presented before you, considering yourself and the way that you work and the goals that you have, and then making an educated decision about what you want to do and how you want to step forward.

You need to be able to know what's ahead in the job market and consider that too. What position and careers will be more in-demand and which will be growing in the years to come. Do any of those appeal to you? Plus, you need to ask other questions too about what you want to achieve, what you want to feel, the sort of person you want to be, and the way that a particular career could add to subtract from your goals.

Lots of questions to juggle, I know. But you're not going to be able to plan your career if you don't ask them.

4 | MAPPING OUT YOUR CAREER PATH

At this point, there is hopefully some image in your mind of the sort of career that you want. Through the use of career clusters, your own dreams and desires, and investing each and every path laid before you, you likely have an idea of what your future may look like and which job could be right for you.

That's great, that's a step above what most people have at this point. Most teeangers aren't thinking about their careers. Instead, they are thinking of jobs that will help them earn a little extra money, pay their phone bills, help them with student debt, or allow them to live comfortably. And while there is nothing wrong with that, you are going to be set up in a much better position than them if you continue down the path you are on.

And that path is your career path. Essentially, it is how you get from Point A to Point B, with Point B being your chosen dream career.

The sad and honest truth is that landing the job you want is not always easy and there are many steps you have to go through to make it happen. But the good news is that you have already done so much of the hard work. You have already put in the effort and the time and the energy to figure out what sort of job will be right for you. That is a huge hurdle that many people your age don't get past.

But now it is time to do the next part. It is time for you to build a career path that will offer you the easiest and smartest and most reasonable and reliable way to start working in your dream job as soon as you can. You don't have to wait until you're in your mid-to-late thirties to have the sort of career that is perfect for you, not if you do the right planning and create your career path while you are still a teeanger.

So, how is it done? Well, like creating any sort of road map or plan, it requires that you put some more energy and thought into where you are heading. But it also requires that you do some observation and research about the world and the job landscape you currently live in and build from that.

SETTING GOALS AND TRACKING YOUR PROGRESS

Like anything in life, you are going to need to set some goals for yourself when it comes to creating your career path and keeping yourself on it. These goals can be updated, tweaked, and changed when you feel it is appropriate.

But this is only going to help you if you are honest with yourself, hold yourself accountable and really deliver on the promises that you make to you. You need to track your progress because this is the best way to determine if you are really delivering on what you need to and keeping yourself on the straight and narrow, headed toward success and the career you have always wanted.

The first step to creating your goals and getting you to meet them is one you are quite familiar with by now: making a checklist.

MAKING A CHECKLIST

It feels like so much of your life is about making checklists right now. Whether that be for a high school project, planning for college, or figuring out what job is right for you and your future, you are always listing out the things that you need to do and then making sure you follow through with them.

But there is a reason why checklists pop up again and again when you are making plans for something, no matter what it is: because they work. If you want to make sure you are doing everything that needs to be done, a checklist is crucial. And make no mistake: you will be doing many things when you are creating your career plan.

What does this career path checklist look like?

You want to sit down and put together a list of all the things that will get you to your dream job. Of course, this means you need to have a good idea of what your dream job is because that will obviously inform the checklist you are making.

EDUCATION

For example, if you have figured out that you want to be a teacher in high school, you know that you will need to reach a certain level of education. Gaining that sort of education would be the first item on your checklist because it's one of the biggest.

Within that box, there will be smaller, important tasks that you will need to reach too. For example, you will have to get enrolled in school for teaching, you will have to buy your books, you will have to figure out your schedule.

As you can see, your checklist will naturally and organically grow and change depending on the path you are going down. But the checklist can't even begin until you have your sights set on a certain type of job.

Your checklist should include other items that are about educating yourself too. Whether it be teaching or another type of job, you need to be sure that you have a solid and deep understanding of the profession, the industry, and what is expected of you. You should read up on the job that you are thinking about, you should become something of an expert about it. And this will be yet another item on your checklist: education.

But education goes beyond just reading. You should reach out to people that you know who have done the same job you are thinking about. Do you want to be an engineer and are close to engineers in your family or close circle of friends? Reach out to them. That is true no matter what the job is. The best way for you to really research the job at hand is to ask about it and there is no one better to ask than the people who work in that job day in and day out.

MAKING CONTACTS

Now, you might not know anyone who works in the job that you're thinking about and that is totally okay. But you can still reach out to people and pick their brains. You can perhaps post on a local page on Facebook, find a message board related to the profession you're thinking of or even visit a local business that specializes in it. Don't be afraid to ask around and inquire with those who know.

Not only does this teach you some important things and mark a huge item off of your checklist, but it will also get you in contact with the people you need to know too. You never know, you might strike up a friendship with someone who already has this job and that is a great way to get a referral for the future. That means that when you are finally looking to apply, you will already have a connection within the industry who can help you make more and get your foot in the door.

MANAGING YOUR FINANCES

A checklist for your career path should also include something that is very important, and sometimes stressful: finances.

You need to know that you are going to have enough money to make ends meet as you are on your journey to your dream job. That means that you might have to work another job, perhaps one you are not crazy about, in order to set up the sort of career you really want.

There are millions of people who grapple with this and, frankly, it's not always that exciting or fun. Think of all the young people you know who are working a part time job so they can have the sort of money needed for college or another job that they are really passionate about. This is just one of the sacrifices that people make in order to really live the life that they want.

In order for you to hold onto the sort of money you need, you have to know what you're going to be spending it on. If you are doing some sort of formal education for your upcoming career, that will play heavily into how much money you need to have. Don't forget how expensive books and classes cost these days!

But you also need to think about transportation, accreditation, research, and more. And of course you have to also consider the amount of money that you need to spend monthly on the bills that you have like rent, cell phone, car, etc.

This part of the checklist is really about financing and balancing your budget. And if you don't have a budget, now is a good time to make one. At this point in your life, having a reliable budget that you take seriously is the key to financial success, no matter what sort of job you have.

Sure, there are things more important than money but no one can deny that money is very vital if you want to live a comfortable life. Having lots of money doesn't make you a better person and it doesn't solve all of the issues that will arise throughout the years.

But there is no doubt that when you have a stable and comfortable bank account, you will feel relaxed and free of anxieties and pressures that bother so many others.

Making money isn't always hard. There are plenty of part time jobs out there that can provide you with the financial well-being you need as you continue down your path for your lifelong career. However, keeping that money can be. It isn't always easy to retain the money that you earn. However, learning how to manage your money is a life skill that everyone should know and there is no better time to learn it than when you are a teenager starting down your career path.

There are people well into their 30s and 40s who sadly don't know the first thing about saving their money. And it shows. They are living paycheck to paychecks, deeply in debt, with little room for improvement or change. They are constantly checking their bank accounts, not sure how they will make ends meet, and living in a state of near-panic at all times. And they are definitely not enjoying their dream jobs. Instead, they are happy and lucky to get any sort of job because they hardly have enough money to get by. They don't have the financial comfort that allows them to really pursue something they are passionate about.

That's not the sort of life you want, right?

Few life skills are as important as being able to manage your money. And learning this skill at a young age, like the age you are now, is very important. That's because you are probably making a good stream of money and you need to know how to deal with it.

If you don't learn how to manage your money as a young adult, you are simply setting yourself up for years of hardships and struggle. Much like learning a musical instrument, these are skills that are best picked up when you are a young person. It's all about making and following habits that you can stick to for the rest of your life.

If you want to save money, you need to be totally honest with yourself about how much money you make and how you spend the income that makes its way into your account.

If you are not very aware of how you spend your cash, you won't be able to save it. We all know the general ways we spend our money. We buy groceries, we pay our bills, we purchase gas for our cars, we sometimes go out and have a nice dinner or movie with friends.

You are going to need to dig deeper into your habits if you wish to start earnestly saving your money.

You have to discover how to reduce your spending if you want to find a way to save money. The good news is that you can easily figure out where your money is going, down to the very last penny. That's because in most bank statements, spending reports are included and they will show you what business and services you are buying with your hard-earned cash.

These reports can give you a clear picture as to where all of your money has been moving to and show you where you might save costs. You can then start to see patterns. Thirty dollars a week on Starbucks coffee? What would happen if you aimed for fifteen a week instead? Are you still paying for that streaming service that you hardly ever use? Are you spending way more on eating out then staying in? Are you paying for a car wash membership during the rainy season?

See, all of this will add up and you will find habits that you can reduce or eliminate. By doing so, you will be saving money. Every dollar not spent on these habits is a dollar saved for the future.

When you really take a good, hard look at your habits, you can find the ones that need to be erased. And when you do that, you will notice that you are soon saving way more money than ever before. You need to be mindful about how you spend and that starts with a solid, in-depth review of how you spend your cash.

And don't forget a budget. One of the most important ways to save money is to create a budget for yourself. This should definitely be on your checklist once you have figured out all the money that you are going to spend in order to make your dream job a reality.

This might seem like a simple step and something that you could master without much research or forethought. You just write down all the money you make and figure out how you're going to spend it in the weeks and months ahead, right?

Well, no, it's not that easy. In fact, it takes a lot more skill than that. Making a good budget, one you can really rely on and one that will serve you well, means understanding what a budget it is and what it does and why you need it.

If you can really grasp what a budget does and what purpose it serves, you will be able to use it to your advantage and get the most of it. So, what is a budget and why do you need one when you are young and money is coming into your bank account so quickly?

When most people think about a budget, they imagine a strict set of rules that is restricting how you can spend your money. They think that a budget is a bunch of ways for limiting you, telling you what you cannot do. But that simply isn't true. People on a budget aren't prohibited from spending their cash as they see fit. In fact, people who use a budget are encouraged to spend and treat themselves and enjoy their lives. They just do it all smart, correctly, and with some proper planning.

A budget is a plan. It's a way of looking at how you need to spend your money and making sure you have enough to make ends meet. But with a budget, you can still go out on the town, you can still go to the movies and buy a new phone and take a vacation and celebrate with friends. You are just doing it all intelligently with forethought.

When you use a budget correctly, you will find that you actually have more freedom and more chances to do things that you love and enjoy. And you won't be sweating every purchase, nervous about the next week and waiting anxiously for the next paycheck.

BREAKING YOUR CHECKLIST DOWN

It's not a bad idea to get very specific about your checklist. In fact, it's very smart to break it down as much as possible.

Instead of large, vague goals that you could complete at any time, get more specific about your job-related goals. Break them down month by month and figure out your checklist and your gameplan for the next thirty days. Go from month-to-month instead of focusing only on the large, overarching big picture.

Some of your goals really might not be time-restricted. That means you can do them at any time. But even if they aren't time-restricted, make them so. Put an artificial but respected timeline for your goals. Even if it doesn't have to be done at a certain time, make it feel like it does.

Your monthly checklist should start small, at first. Give yourself just three or four tasks that you have to get done by a certain date. And as time goes on, make that list grow until you are doing more and more for each and every month. Before you know it, you'll be well ahead of schedule.

A checklist is important because it's all about keeping yourself accountable. And if you are trying to land the dream job that you have always wanted, being accountable is beyond paramount. It's perhaps the most important thing when it comes to job-hunting. Why? Because no one is going to just hand you a job. No one is going to give you a career. You have to work hard for it and you have to prove you can do it and you have to show others that you're the right person for the job. And you can only do that if you hold yourself to a very high standard and demand a lot from yourself.

That is what a checklist does: it sets goals for you by you. It makes you force yourself to be the sort of person and employee that businesses will race to hire. It is about pushing yourself and proving yourself, not just to others but to yourself as well.

SITTING DOWN WITH OTHERS

Speaking of accountability, sometimes you need others to keep you on track and make sure you are following the goals that you have set for yourself. This means that you may need to call upon others to help you out.

Maybe you have a mentor whose judgment you trust. Perhaps that mentor is a teacher or a family friend. Whoever it is, you should try to schedule regular meetings with them to assess your goals and your progress.

Try to sit down with this person just once a month at the start and lay out what you are planning, what you want to achieve, and where you ideally see yourself in a few months. Let them give you feedback, pointers, advice, and critiques. And listen to all of it very closely.

The advice they give might be eye-opening. They could tell you that you're doing things perfectly but they could also say that maybe you're biting off more than you can chew or that maybe you're not putting enough on your plate. You need to consider what they tell you. Remember, you choose them as the person that you sit down with, your mentor of sorts. So you should only select someone whose ideas you value and opinion you trust.

Make sure that this person of your choosing is someone you want to be like. They don't have to necessarily work in the field that you are pursuing but they should be someone who has created the sort of life and career that you admire and want for yourself.

Just like you are always going to be honest with yourself about your career path and plans, you need to be honest with this person too. You need to tell them the shortcomings you encountered, the things you achieved, what was easier and what was harder. Are you having doubts about the path you are on? Tell them. Even if it is something monumental and scary, like perhaps changing your destined career, you need to let them know. Getting the words out and expressing yourself will help you make the right choice and open you up to some great feedback and advice that could go a long way to making things easier and more achievable.

Think of this person as a sounding board, someone to bounce ideas off of and collaborate with. This will be your career, of course, but the input you receive at this point could be crucial to helping you make the right choice, stay on track, and perhaps change your approach to landing the job that you have always wanted.

So much of this entire process is interior. It's mostly about what you want, what you feel, what you hope to achieve. But this part of the process is about opening up, reaching out to others, and really sharing yourself in a vulnerable and special way. That is why it's such an important part.

ADJUST YOUR GOALS ACCORDINGLY

You have input from others and, of course, you have your own opinion to think about when it comes to your search for a job.

All of this should be considered as you push forward and try to find your career. But you should also keep something else in mind: changing your mind or adjusting your goals.

There is nothing wrong with tweaking your plan. It is *your* plan, after all. If you feel that something isn't working or that you aren't doing enough of something - or too much of something else - sit down and figure out which adjustments are needed.

BUILDING YOUR CREDENTIALS

Experience is one of among the most crucial factors in career planning. as a teenager.

Without experience, how can you tell what sorts of work you will enjoy? Plus, having experience might make it simpler for you to land the sorts of employment you'll like in the future. Experience may not only aid in job preparation but also improve your résumé, assist with college applications, and teach you more about yourself. Consider volunteer work, work experience, guidance, and self-directed learning. Ensure that you are aware of and ready for the schooling needed for the vocation you have chosen.

EXPERIENCE

The significance of having a job is virtually always mentioned in career events for high school pupils. It is crucial for you as a teenager to have work experience since it will make finding employment much simpler in the future. It might also assist you in developing an understanding of what various types of employment entail.

You're most likely to find entry-level employment as a teenager in the retail and customer service sectors. Even while they may not be the sorts of occupations you want to pursue in the future, they may show prospective employers that you have experience and teach you how to behave professionally.

Even if you shouldn't be concerned if the jobs you can apply for aren't in your preferred sector, you should be open to any chances that could present themselves in fields of interest. Every high school work experience is vital, but odd or really intriguing employment may provide you a competitive advantage in the future.

VOLUNTEERING

High school students may gain a lot of career exposure and build their resumes by participating in volunteer work. Also, volunteering may provide you the opportunity to work in your chosen industry more than finding employment will. You can find volunteer opportunities by exploring the possibilities and determining the kind of volunteer work that would best suit your needs and advance your own objectives. Independent of your personal job objectives, volunteering may also help you engage with your community and make a difference.

RESEARCHING

Doing your own study is an excellent method to gain experience relevant to the occupations you want. Browse books on the topic at your local library or read about occupations that interest you online. Understand the background of the profession you have chosen as well as the current trends in that industry. Is the sector expanding? Is it contracting? What type of training is usually necessary? You may have a realistic and well-informed assessment of your chances by being as knowledgeable as you can be about your hobbies.

Speaking with others who work in the fields you're interested in is another approach to learn more about them. These folks could be able to serve as mentors for you, sharing their own experiences and providing priceless insights into your available possibilities.

Develop your own experiences in the area of your choice. Observe related places, businesses, and organizations. To demonstrate your interest in a subject, create your personal passion projects or compile a portfolio of your work. Do your best to carve out some extra time for this type of investigation and interaction. It might end up being quite beneficial in the long run.

EDUCATION

Education is the final kind of experience that you should give significant consideration to. What type of schooling is necessary for your desired career? Before your senior year of high school, you must begin making plans for college. It can entail selecting the appropriate high school courses; for instance, many colleges will require certain math or scientific classes for admissions to particular faculties. If your employment requires you to go to college, be sure to submit the best possible application.

It is crucial to give your college applications considerable consideration. You must attend a school that accommodates both your personal requirements and your academic and career needs. You could also have selected a profession that doesn't call for a college degree; for many people, these lines of work can be rewarding, secure, and exciting. If so, you might want to consider submitting an application to a trade or vocational school.

Make sure you are ready for the application process regardless of the level of schooling that is required for the job you have chosen. Consider seeking career counseling for high school kids through your school or community center if you believe you need it.

OTHER ELEMENTS TO CONSIDER

Each has distinct demands and life situations, which will affect their career and possibilities. You may create a profession for yourself that is unique to you by completely comprehending your own wants. While making your decision, you should also take the job market into account; certain occupations have a better future than others, which may affect the kind of employment you choose to pursue. Being truthful about your desires, requirements, duties, and possibilities, as well as the occupations that could fit with those characteristics, is essential for effective career evaluation for high school students.

Your Personal Life

A person's professional decisions may be influenced by several life events, both positive and negative. This is not to argue that if you lead a specific life, you aren't qualified for some occupations. But everyone has certain things going on in their lives that influence the choices they make and what is reasonably available to them.

While making plans and selecting occupations, you must take into account conditions that are beyond your control. This is what consideration of your situation entails. Becoming aware of any obstacles that your dream profession may present due to circumstances that are out of your control can help you discover solutions and lead the life you want.

The Work Market

When your parents first started working, the employment economy was different from what it is now. The types of occupations that are offered also alter as a result of the constant change in the world. It is in your best interests to explore in-demand careers to choose the potential best career options. There are alternatives for you to pursue your interests if the profession you had your heart set on is no longer feasible.

Maybe you've always wanted to work in a field like newspaper journalism, which is becoming less and less in demand and available. You might need to alter your objectives; attempt to land a job with a well-known website instead.

Your Time Off

Right now, you are young. This means that you want to actually enjoy your life and not just be making plans for the future. You want to get out there, hang with your friends, go on vacations, see the world, and actually make memories that you will remember for a lifetime.

Sometimes, pursuing a career can get in the way of that and it is important that you balance your personal life with the career path that you are crafting for yourself. And you should consider this balance when you are mapping out your path forward. You should think about how much time you'll want off, the sort of things you'll want to do, the life experiences you'll want to enjoy, and how all of this fits in with your career aspirations.

There is nothing wrong with you wanting to be young and enjoy yourself. In fact, if you are able to do this then it's actually more likely that you'll also be able to thrive in the career that you choose. Studies have shown that people who are happy outside of work are almost always better employees, work harder, reach for more, and thrive in their professional environment. So you should absolutely embrace your desire to enjoy your life. But you just need to figure out a way to do that *and* follow your career aspirations and dreams.

Your Current - and Future - Location
Some jobs are solely dependent on your location.

You might find a job that is perfect for you, the sort of career that you can see yourself enjoying for decades until you retire. But it also might require that you are in a certain place, a particular region or city.

Although many companies allow and embrace remote working now, there are some that are still old-fashioned and want you to show up, in person, to your job every single workday. And if you are pursuing a job like that then you need to think about where you live. Are you hoping to settle down with a business that needs you to live in one city? Can you commit to that sort of move? Can you afford it? And what about the future? Can you always envision yourself staying in one place or do you want to move around the country, even the world, as you grow older?

This isn't as common a problem as it used to be but it's still pressing for many people. And if this applies to you, you need to be honest with yourself about where you are now and where you imagine you could be in the future. If your location is bound to change, that is okay. But it may exclude you from having certain jobs. As always, be honest about what you want from your life. You are young now, your plans may change. But you should consider where you are living and where you are willing - and not willing - to work in the future when you are hunting for your future career.

Opportunities
The potential for professional growth and development is a crucial element to take into account while making career decisions. Will a certain occupation allow you to grow over the years, or are you more likely to hit a brick wall after a few years?

In contrast to others, certain professions provide a wide range of prospects for progression.

For instance, many business environments give the opportunity to advance into managerial positions from entry-level employment. In contrast, there is sometimes minimal opportunity for growth in occupations that are paid hourly. Some professions, like entrepreneurship, provide limitless room for advancement.

Evaluate a potential professional path's potential for growth and advancement as you consider your possibilities.

Job Benefits

Benefits packages differ significantly from one firm to the next, thus it is wise to compare what different organizations provide. One might allow you to work from your house or pay for your internet, whereas others don't. While seeking employment, it's important to take everything like this into account.

And, of course, professions also allow employees to enjoy other benefits such as health insurance too. And within that benefit, there are many intricate and important distinctions, such as what the insurance plans cover and what you have to pay for out of pocket.

Although companies are unlikely to be capable of competing on salaries, they could be able to do so on benefits. For instance, even if jobs are available at a somewhat lesser compensation than others, the ability to work from home can be a top priority on your list of requirements. That could be enough to sway you to pursue a job, even if the pay isn't exactly what you had in mind.

Benefits play an important part in a job hunt and they can be the determining factor for many people. Think of which benefits are important to you. Think of the ones that are required for you to even consider taking on a job.

HOW TO MAKE YOUR CAREER PATH STRONGER & EASIER

TAKE SPECIALIZED CLASSES

You might be tired of taking classes at this point in your life because you have spent years upon years in school, taking various classes, tests, and more. But the truth is that taking *more* classes is actually a really good and beneficial way to enhance your skills, become a better employee, and find the right career for you.

There are various possibilities accessible today via classes that can tailor to the specific needs that you have for the career of your choice. Some jobs require that you attend certain classes or receive specific classifications and certifications.

These special classes are just about everywhere. Although four-year universities give the chance to study a particular topic in detail and earn a bachelor's degree, community colleges also offer affordable courses and associate graduate schools. Meanwhile, professional certifications educate people in a particular skill area, like the afore-mentioned cybersecurity.

Online learning options are also provided by several institutions of higher learning. There are now numerous sites online that will help you study and develop a certain craft. Most of them require a fee and that you attend an amount of hours in an online course. For your hard work, you will be accredited with the certification and completion of the class, which will be respected by the industry you are trying to enter.

GET A WORK PERMIT

If you are starting your career earlier than most people, that means you might need a work permit in order to be employed by a certain company. This varies from state to state, and even from company to company. But if you require a work permit, seek one out. In most states, a permit like this is needed for anyone under 18 years old.

Therefore, you might need to get a work permit before beginning employment with some businesses or governmental organizations. These criteria frequently change depending on the field you wish to work in, where you live, and how old you are. To determine if you need to submit a work permit application, research the regulations for your location and sector.

Check out a useful state-by-state guide to work permits provided by the U.S. Department of Labor on their website to see if you need this permit.

You will then have to reach out to the school that you're attending. That is because, typically, state labor departments and school guidance counselors give out work permits to teens. The guidance counselors at your school ought to be prepared to respond to any questions and are most likely to have work permit forms available.

What will you need when you want to apply for a work permit? It is a fairly easy process but it does require a few important documents that you or your parents should have.

You will have to fill out an application that will ask for your personal information, such as your social security number, your date of birth, and more. You will also need a recent physical or a doctor's note, as well as a document like a birth certificate, passport, driver's license, or state-issued photo ID card.

Finally, you'll need the signature of your parents, agreeing to you receiving your work permit.

Once you have acquired your permit, there might still be some regulations that you have to follow related to your new job. For example, some states require that anyone under 18 only work during certain hours. This might be good for you because it'll mean less late nights. But there are other things related to the physical work you can do, and the rate you can be paid, that are restricted by your age.

Receiving your work permit as a teenager is a huge step forward and a key to finding a job at a young age.

CREATE YOUR RESUME

You may be aiming for a job in a field that doesn't require a resume but there is a chance that you still need one. Whether it's just getting your foot in the door with a part time job or your chosen dream job does need one, you should always have a good - and updated - resume on hand.

This means that you should absolutely write your resume now. Because even if you don't need one, having a resume will increase your chances of landing a job. How should someone just starting out on their career path a resume?

What is a resume? It is essentially a typed letter that showcases all of the work experience you have had in your life. And if you haven't had many jobs, your resume will teach a possible employer about the things you will bring to the job, from experience to hobbies to other strong suits that could make you a wonderful worker who could help them.

You will probably need to include additional information, such as relevant education, extracurricular activities, and volunteer experience, as you have a limited amount of work experience. Being a teenager means that you'll have to get a bit clever when you are creating your resume. To obtain some insight into what a strong one should contain, it might be useful to look at student and resume samples.

No matter your age or your experience, your resume certainly needs to include some pertinent information, such as your education and contact information. Beyond that, you can have a little bit of fun. You should emphasize non-work activities that could make you appealing for a job, such as babysitting, sports you have played, clubs you have been in, and volunteer work you have committed.

It's also extra important that you portray yourself as a strong leader, someone who can get a lot of work done and help others do the same. Employers, no matter their industry, want to only hire people who will make life easier for them - and more productive too. A proven team leader is someone who can make life much easier for a business. He or she can raise ships across the water.

Have you been the leader in a student government program? Perhaps you have been the captain of a sports team? All of this should be accounted for and written about - and it could all have an impact on how you look.

It's also vital that you don't write anything too complicated or over the top. You should make it fairly basic, easy to understand, and straightforward. Use a simple format and a font that is easy to visualize and see. There are countless resume templates on the internet that you can use and most of them will advise that you use fonts like Arial, Calibri, Times New Roman, or others.

When you are writing your resume, think about what the possible employer you're applying for wants. There is nothing wrong with tailoring your resume for a specific job. That means that you might have multiple resumes saved, based on the several jobs you could be thinking about pursuing. For each job, play up the responsibilities and skills that you have that are more attractive for that position.

There are also things called "action words" that are very important when you are creating your resume. These words will pop on the page and really speak to what your possible employer is looking for. Think of words like "created", "led", "researched", "experienced", and others. All of these speak about someone who is proactive, works hard, and has helped others achieve their goals over the years.

It is also incredibly vital that you read over your resume - often! If you leave it filled with misspellings and errors then you are really just shooting yourself in the foot and doing more harm than good. You need to always remember that your resume is a reflection of you and if it isn't looking good and professional, *you* aren't looking good and professional. Remember that this is the first thing that a potential employer will see from you. This is your first impression, so you better make it count.

Finally, make sure that you have plenty of references in your resume. A reference is just someone who is going to vouch for you and testify that you are a good employee, a hard worker, and worthy of being hired. Think of teachers who have had an impact on your life, family friends, or even people who have coached you or worked with you in clubs or activities outside of school. Make sure you include their up-to-date contact information because many jobs will in fact reach out to your references.

One more thing about a resume: since you are young, you might have an email account that reflects your youthful and fun personality. But you should remember that this sort of email address, while appropriate for friends reaching out to you, might not be great for a job. If your email address includes curse words, slang, or anything remotely inappropriate, you shouldn't use it. Instead, create a new email address that is specifically made for your job-hunting.

Also, it's not a bad idea to include a cover letter with your resume. This is simply what it sounds like" a letter that basically sums you up and describes what you are looking for and hoping to achieve. This isn't written in bullet points and brief statements like your resume. Instead, it is written in basic prose, just like any other letter would be.

Make sure you use those action words again throughout the cover letter because this is the best place for you to summarize your personality and the atmosphere and attitude that you would bring to any business that you are applying for.

CONCLUSION

A lot of work has to be put into mapping out the career path that is right for you.

Far too many people believe that once they settle on the job of their dreams, the work to get it is easy and will go without a hitch. But that's not true. In fact, figuring out which job feels right for you is just the first step.

Once you have determined which career is the one that you can best thrive at, you have to do the hard work of creating your path to get it. This starts with you setting your goal, making a checklist, conferring with others, and adjusting those goals.

You should also think of ways to make yourself a stronger employee and, therefore, your career path stronger too. This includes doing things such as taking classes, thinking of what you can and cannot accept when it comes to pay, benefits, and more, and also create a resume that will do a great job at selling yourself to your potential employer. If you need a work permit or a certification, now would be the time to get those as well.

All of this will come together and turn you into the sort of hard-working, driven, and beneficial employee that any number of companies would be eager to acquire.

5 | HIGH SCHOOL EDUCATION PLAN

Thinking about career planning when you're just a teenager might be overwhelming. That is because you already have just so much on your plate and so many things that you are trying to do.

You are attempting to make friends, keep a strong relationship with your family members, get good grades, and have some semblance of a life outside of school too. That's a lot for anyone! And to add career planning on top of that is just making a tricky situation even trickier.

In order to be good at career planning, you have to be good at school too. The two go together, hand-in-hand. If you aren't accomplishing a lot in school, you will not turn yourself into the sort of young adult who businesses will want to hire. Instead, you'll lack drive and attention to detail and the ability to work well on your own or also with a team.

As much as you may not like to admit it, high school is important because of the way that it makes you into the young adult you're meant to be. But that is only true if you make the best of your high school years, really use them to your advantage, and try hard to get the most out of them.

That means, yet again, some planning is necessary. If you plan accordingly and handle high school with the right mindset, you will leave at the end of it as a strong, committed, smart, and capable young person who is ready to not only conquer your career, but also the world.

So, what do you need to do during your high school years? Let's take a deep look into how you can accomplish the most during these four years.

EARLY HIGH SCHOOL (9–10TH GRADE)

Freshman year: it's a new beginning and a chance for you to meet new people, decide upon your goals, and rediscover the type of person you are and the type of person you wish to be.

Yes, your first year in high school is a very big one and it honestly freaks some people out because they feel the weight and pressure of it all pressing down upon them. There is no mistaking the fact that a lot rides on your freshman year, but it doesn't need to overwhelm or frighten you. Think of it as a giant opportunity, a chance for you to stake out on a new path, one that will lead to your adulthood and your career. Freshman year doesn't have to be full of challenges, it is full of chances.

What is the first thing you should focus on in your opening year of high school? It's a pretty simple one: learning the ins and outs of your high school and figuring out how it worked.

GET TO KNOW YOUR SCHOOL

Prior to starting your first year in high school, you should try to attend any type of orientation that is offered to incoming ninth graders. During this time, you should explore the buildings as best as you can. Not only should you pay attention to the parts of the school where your classes will be, but also figure out where your locker is, where the offices are, and where the lunchroom and bathrooms are too. You are going to be spending a lot of time in this school so you should know it inside and out like the back of your hand.

By the time your first day begins, you'll know just where you're going, as well as other places of interest throughout your school. But orientation will do more than that too. You will also meet a few people, such as your other classmates and the teachers of the school too. This will put you at ease, make you feel less alone, and might even lead to a few budding friendships before the bell rings on the first day of school.

CHOOSE YOUR CLASSES

High school gives you more chances to choose your classes and dictate your path through your educational process. Through electives, you are able to select some of the classes that you are signed up for.

At this point, the idea of going easy on yourself might sound appealing. Imagine just being able to coast through high school without breaking much of a sweat. But while that might feel easier to you and create less challenges, it's actually not better for you in the long run and won't help you graduate with good grades, experience, and also set yourself up for a strong career in your chosen field.

You should try to challenge yourself when you are picking your classes. Don't overwhelm yourself and put too much on your plate, but you should certainly think of the big picture and what is going to be best for you as a student and a young adult looking to start a career in a few years.

If there were certain classes that really challenged you in junior high school, you should be sure that you take a few in high school that will make you stronger in those areas, turning you into a fully fleshed-out student with few weak spots. Additionally, each and every semester during high school should have at least one class that revolves around a future career that you are interested in. This will keep building your skills and continue you down a path that will ultimately lead you to the job that you want.

GET YOURSELF ORGANIZED

High school is going to put a lot on your plate, much more than you were used to during your years in junior high and before. You will have more textbooks, more tests, more assignments, more activities, and many more responsibilities.

If you don't take the time to inspect and improve your organizational skills then you are going to end up making high school much, much harder on yourself. From the ways that you file your pens into your backpack to the methods that you set reminders for yourself, you need to come up with a system that will last you not only through these next four years, but the rest of your life as well.

Think of all of the dates that you will need to keep track of, all of the assignment responsibilities that you will need to stay on top of. All of these are vital and you will need to work on your work ethic to make sure they are all addressed and never forgotten.

Stay True To Yourself & Figure Out Who You Are

High school will be a time period in your life when you are meeting many new people and enjoying new experiences. That means that you could possibly get confused about who you are, what you want, and what is best for you.

The sad truth is that there are many students who don't make the best out of high school and run into a lot of problems with their lives. They start slacking in class and start paying more attention to their friends and having fun out of school instead of getting good grades and finding success in the classroom.

You need to be very careful at this point in your high school career to ensure that you are making the right choices and going down the smartest path. Don't let distractions pull you down, such as partying or hanging out with friends instead of studying or even more serious and dangerous choices. While there will certainly be a time for having fun and being close with your friends, it all needs to be balanced and you should never lose track of the greater good: being the best student you can be so you can be on the right path for your career when high school concludes.

You are going to learn a lot about yourself during your high school years. You'll discover your likes and dislikes, the things you want to try and the things that are of no interest to you. You'll also meet friends, some of whom will be with you through thick and thin through the rest of your life.

High school is not just a journey through your classes and studies, it is a journey of self-discovery too. It is an avenue for you to figure out so much about yourself, who you are, and the sort of person you are going to be.

Now, don't get too overwhelmed when thinking about that. Don't let it frighten you too much. This will all come naturally if you let it. Just trust in yourself, don't let yourself go down a bad path, and remember the potential that you have and the path that you are one. This will all be exciting.

CONNECT WITH OLDER KIDS

At this point in your high school career, it's not uncommon for you to feel out of sorts, in the deep end, and not sure what steps to take next to find success. If only there were other people who had been there before, navigating through all of this, and made it out to the other side.

Well, good news: there are. You can actually make connections and friendships with older students who can help you stay on the right path and keep your best foot forward through your four years of school.

In certain schools, a mentoring program pairs freshmen with seniors. But, ninth graders also can take the attempt of getting to know an upperclassman on their own, such as a friend's older sister, a neighbor, a club or teammate.

Remember that the older students were once freshmen as well. It's not as if this is something that has never happened before. There are people who are willing to share their experiences, offer advice, and be helpful.

Reaching out to an older student can be even easier if you have a sibling who is one. Feel free to talk to your older brother or sister and seek assistance and guidance about what you should be doing and expecting in your first years of high school. They will likely give you the best advice because they have been in the same spot you are now but they also know you very well and understand you better than most anyone else. They will keep this in mind when giving you the sort of advice that you need.

USE ACTIVITIES TO MAKE FRIENDS

Although you will be going to high school in order to study and pass your classes, there are many other things that you can do when you are going through these important four years of your young life. And one of the things that can most benefit you is the inner-school activities that cannot only pump up your college application and, therefore, your future career but also your list of friends.

High schools have a variety of events all year long, such as athletic competitions, musical performances, plays, and pep rallies. If possible, participate in these events. Attend with friends or take advantage of the chance to socialize with other students. Joining a club, honor society, or volunteering are other ways to meet your classmates.

Discover a solution to shrink the size of the enormous campus community. To improve your college application, don't simply join a bunch of groups, as this might result in fatigue. Choose a chosen handful of things you are interested in instead. If you are just ticking boxes for college admissions, the authorities will know that and will see right through you. Thus, be thoughtful about how you spend your time.

GET CLOSE WITH TEACHERS & STAFF

Students typically rush out of the classroom as soon as the bell sounds. Therefore, spend the time after school getting to know your professors and guidance counselors. Having such connections may help with the adjustment and ultimately be beneficial, especially when you start to apply to institutions.

Teachers frequently go to kid-related activities, whether they be sporting or performing arts events. Be careful to say hello to your instructor if you run into them at a gathering. Say "thank you" to them since they are standing by your side and care about your success.

FOCUS ON YOUR OWN MENTAL HEALTH

There will be a lot going on during your four years in high school and much of it is very important. However, nothing is as important as taking care of yourself. And when it comes to taking care of yourself, it's not just about making sure you aren't getting physically ill or hurting yourself. It's also about making sure you are paying close attention to your mental health and how you are feeling emotionally.

Mental health matters have, thankfully, become more prominent in the media and society lately and more and more people are paying attention to them. However, there is still quite a ways to go and more work to be done.

As reported by the CDC, millions of students suffered greatly because of the coronavirus and the shutdown that ensued because of it. About 40% of high school students had poor mental health throughout the COVID-19 pandemic. High school pupils who identify as female or LGBTQ are more likely than their peers to report feeling depressed or hopeless recently.

The bad news is that there will likely be times when you are feeling down in the dumps, low energy, or just not 100% mentally. This happens to everyone and it's definitely probably that some moments in your high school career will be impaired by this. The good news is that the majority of educational institutions have mental health resources that are accessible, namely counselors, therapists, and social workers, so experts advise kids not to be reluctant to ask for help. There is help out there for you, you just have to know how to reach out and get it. And reaching out isn't that hard when you are in high school. If you are ever feeling any way that alarms you, you will be accepted with open arms by the professionals working at your school, ready to assist you.

Between your freshman year of high school and your senior year, a lot of significant emotions occur. The amount of development that occurs in simply your body is enormous. Thus, look after your emotional, bodily, and social well-being. You must pay close attention to your emotional well-being. Mental health matters can be tricky and they have a way of sliding to the back burner because you have just so many things to deal with. But ignoring how you feel emotionally is a very bad idea and can lead to you doing poorly in class and, even worse, in life too.

Learning how to handle your emotional issues at this age is a very smart idea because it lays the foundation for years and years of being introspective and caring for yourself. This is when you will learn habits that you will use for the rest of your years. If you learn in high school to take care of how your mind is doing, you will keep this habit up in the years to come. It'll last you beyond your years in high school, and college. It'll be something that you value and are good at for the rest of your life.

Additionally, you need to work hard at staying in the here and now and not let your mind wander too far into the future. If you do, you'll find out that you have missed out on some of the biggest moments in your high school tenure. Some pupils have their sights set on college even before they start high school. Nonetheless, remain present and enjoy your four years of high school.

If you're having a difficult day, keep in mind that it only lasts for 24 hours. It's just a fleeting moment before you move on. Cherish your time in high school. Find methods to make it spectacular.

MID HIGH SCHOOL (10–11TH GRADES)

At this point in your high school career, it is time to just stay the course.

During your first years of school, you are still figuring yourself out, settling down, and getting into the groove of being in high school. You are balancing the hard work of classes, studying, making and keeping friends, and also planning what is going to be ahead for you after you graduate. You have an eye on your college choices as well as your career path that is after that.

Staying the course isn't always that easy. In fact, you might not even be entirely sure what it means. Basically, what staying the course is is you doing what you have been doing for the last two years, but just doing it better and more consistently.

Staying the course and preparing for what comes next. One goes with the other during your junior year. If you aren't staying the course and doing as you have been then you won't be able to make formative plans for the future.

So, what should your junior year be full of? What should you be paying attention to and accomplishing as you grow closer to your senior year? What choices will help you get selected by a good college but also prepare you for what comes after that: your career?

KEEP DOING YOUR WORK

Now is not the time to start slacking and going easy on yourself and your work schedule. In fact, your junior year of high school is when you should be working even harder on your work and making a routine that you can stick with. This is because the work that you are doing during this year is more important when it comes to college admissions and setting yourself up for long-term success in the professional world.

Remember, you are creating habits that you'll use for the rest of your life. If you start to become laid back and lazy now, you might be that way for years into your adulthood and that doesn't bode well for your career.

Here is a little secret that many people don't tell you about high school: you are not actually required to be exceptionally smart to accomplish tons while you are in school. You only need to turn up and complete the assignments, including the readings, essays, and puzzles. Now, that's the important part right there: you *have* to get all of your work done if you want to succeed. That might mean that you need to formulate and stick with a schedule that makes you the best sort of hard worker.

This is important because it'll get your projects and assignments done but it's also very important because it will ensure that this is the sort of attitude and drive that you carry into your college career and beyond.

Make doing the work your first priority during your sophomore and junior year in high school. The rest will take care of itself. Most experts agree that it is better if you study each day at the identical time and location. 4 PM in your bedroom. 3:30 in the school's library. 4:30 in your family's den. It doesn't matter where you chose to get your work done, just make sure that you are adamant about doing it from the same place, at the same time, each and every day.

Even though some days might go more smoothly than others, sticking to a daily plan, including on weekends, can help you stay on track. Not only will it prove to you to be more efficient and consistent but it will also create those good habits that will help you in the long run.

Many college students say that they actually didn't spend too much time doing homework in the years before entering their university. In light of the fact that many college freshmen claim they never completed more than an hour of homework every day in high school, two hours of homework should offer you a market edge and a relaxed sense of confidence. In the grand scheme of things, that's not too much time so you can definitely fit it in your regular daily schedule.

But you should find whatever works for you. Maybe you need to take a break during your homework schedule. Or maybe you have some household chores that are going to get in the way every day. Therefore, if you believe you require a three-hour block, that is totally fine. Whatever works for you is what you need to pursue. Nevertheless, spending the entire two hours each day and getting ahead of schedule when you run out of daily tasks can provide dividends that will astound you.

GETTING INTO A GOOD COLLEGE ISN'T TOO HARD

Here is yet another secret that not enough parents or teachers tell you when you are in high school: if you are determined to do so, you *can* get into a college. And even if you don't make it to Harvard or Yale or another Ivy League school, you can still get into a college that will do quite well for you and give you a premium education that will last a lifetime.

The truth is that you have more college and university options in this country than in any other nation in the globe, even though it might not be a school that your family is aware of. Have you seen how many young people are relocating to the United States to pursue their studies? They are aware that all you need to succeed academically in the United States is a fundamental command of English and a commitment to hard effort.

You should absolutely have your favorite schools in mind and set your sights high. If you are a good student and have worked hard throughout your high school career, there is a good chance that you can make it into one of these schools. Yet, even if you aren't accepted to the top of the top, don't give up hope and lose faith. Don't assume that you won't have a college education because you've been passed up by some of the top schools in the nation.

There are plenty of ways for you to still get a great, top of the line education. You can elect to go to a community college, and then transfer to a four-year school. Or you can choose a lesser-known but still accomplished university from across the country. Your choices are plenty and you shouldn't throw your hands up in the air and just think that all is lost if you haven't been accepted by the best of the best right away. As time has gone on, more colleges have been established and they all offer great educational choices for you.

Most universities accept the majority of their applications, but some reputable ones still have open spots in September. No matter where you are aiming to attend, do not lose faith if things don't go your way right away.

But make no mistake: it is important that you make it into a university if you are planning to create a strong career path for yourself. Although a college education isn't as helpful as it once was when it comes to landing a fulltime job, it is still something that many businesses, including high-end ones, require if you are trying to get a job. And, frankly, any education at college is better than no education. If you don't go to college at all, you will find that some businesses won't even look at your resume in the future. So you should definitely make sure that you are accepted to a college after high school.

DON'T FREAK OUT ABOUT THE SATS

Some young people your age put a lot of pressure on themselves to do incredibly well on the SAT and ACT tests. They feel that these tests are make-or-break when it comes to getting into college and, therefore, setting themselves up for a long and fruitful career.

Yes, you've been taught to believe that your chances of getting into college depend on how well you do on the SAT or ACT by the businesses that provide test-prep courses as well as many of your teachers and peers. Simply said, that is untrue. What *is* true is that you can succeed if you complete your assignments, focus in class, and review a couple of the practice exams.

These tests are important, there is no doubt about that. But they are not nearly as vital and life-changing as some people make them out to be. And if you put too much pressure on yourself to do exceedingly well with these tests then you run the risk of freaking yourself out and buckling under all that pressure.

Even if you don't knock the ball out of the park with your SAT and ACT scores, you can still have a long and beneficial time in college. It is true that you have a chance of receiving an acceptance letter from Yale if your SAT or ACT score is in the 2000s or the 30s. But with a lesser score, you will still have more chances to enroll in reputable institutions that welcome students who share your interests. There are good colleges that are pleased with a SAT score of at least 1500 and an ACT score of at least 20.

As mentioned before, you still have plenty of collegiate options before you no matter what choice you take or how well you do in school. While you should certainly study and prepare to take these once-a-year tests, you should also not freak out if you don't do as well as you had hoped. Options still exist and you cannot give up on yourself!

GO TO BED AT A REGULAR TIME

As a teenager, you probably feel more tired than people older than you. Your parents might even give you a hard time about just how much you can sleep and how fatigued you seem to be at all times. But there is a reason for that! Beyond the amount of stuff you have on your plate and just how much work that you have to do in high school, your body is still going through physical changes that can lead to being downright sleepy, even when you have given yourself a lot of time to rest.

But you can always set yourself up for feeling more restful by being mindful about how much sleep you need, and affording yourself that time.

You can reduce the occasional fatigue you experience by going to bed at the same, sensible hour each night. When you think about it, nothing is really worth losing sleep at this age. Hanging out with your friends is definitely fun but it won't be enjoyable if you are hardly able to keep your eyes open. Sleep is refreshing and feels good and it makes sense to get as much of it as you need. Moreover, why stay up late if you have already accomplished all of your tasks and homework?

You're not impressing anyone by not giving yourself the proper amount of rest. Monitor your body, feel out what is an appropriate amount of rest, and go to great lengths to make sure you award it to yourself.

Sleeping should be something that you look forward to after a long, busy, productive day. Make it a wonderful routine that you are excited about. Get in bed with a book you want to read about anything unrelated to school rather than staying up until the wee hours of the morning to contact your buddies and scroll through TikTok.

DON'T DO TOO MANY EXTRACURRICULAR ACTIVITIES

You are young, driven, and have tons of energy. That means that you might feel like you can do multiple things at all times. You can have your hands in multiple pots and still have energy to do more. But is it really smart to commit to tons of different events and clubs at one time? The answer is definitely not.

In fact, it's not a good idea to join your school's theater club, debate team, and volleyball team, as well as choir, Key Club, and volunteering every week at the food bank. That's a lot of activities. In fact, that is just too many activities.

Why is doing so much a bad thing, especially when we have told you to stay involved in your school and extracurricular activities? Honestly, the reasons are endless. Firstly, if you are doing too much at one time, the quality that you put out is bound to suffer. There is no way that you can be so great at everything at all times. Eventually, something has to give. Whether it be your school work or something that you are required to do for one of your many clubs, you won't always be able to give 100% to all things at all times.

Secondly, you will give yourself a very serious case of burn out and that is the fastest and most assured way to run out of energy and fall into a serious funk. If you are burned out, you won't want to do well at school or at work or planning or anything. In fact, you literally won't have the ability to do so. Your body will be exhausted and won't allow you to perform as you wish. Burnout is very real, even for a young and driven person like yourself.

Finally, this doesn't help you when it comes to landing a good college and, after that, a good career too. The truth is that thick resumes are not what the universities are looking for. They need proof of intense love for just a few certain hobbies. Schools will be alarmed and alerted if they see an application that is jam-packed with seemingly endless activities, clubs, and commitments. This shows that the young person applying is someone who is spread too thin, incapable of saying no to people, and ultimately doesn't know what they want to do with themselves. That is not the sort of student that most schools want.

As long as you are fully committed to each of them, just one or two or maybe three activities are just fine. Choose only a select enjoyable activities that you like doing and concentrate solely on them. Enter your work in a nearby event if you enjoy art. Create a regular jam session with acquaintances if you play music. Write in your spare time or donate your energy to your church or local theater. Think about quality over quantity when you are finding things to do outside of your regular day-to-day schooling schedule.

You might feel that you are the best at multitasking but attempting to do everything all at once when you are junior in high school isn't going to help you get into a better college and it's definitely not going to assist you in landing the job of your dreams after that.

SPEND TIME WITH YOUR FRIENDS

The last thing that you want to do when you are so concentrated on school and college and your future career is to forget about the people closest to you: your friends.

One of the most important things that you should do during your junior year is keep your friends close. Far too many teenagers get bogged down with the amount of work they have to do as they plan their job future and their time in college. By the time they graduate, they are excited for what's ahead but they feel like they have missed out on close relationships with their friends. Is all this hard work and planning really worth giving up such vital and heartfelt time with those people who mean the most to you?

While working is important and planning is also vital if you are trying to create a career path for yourself, you also need to ensure that you carve out enough time to hang out with your friends. And when you hang out with them, do it in person. Additionally, don't use this time to talk about classes and job applications and planning.

Instead, use this time to avoid worrying about the world or what lies ahead for you all in college and beyond, try to spend as much time as possible with your friends. Spend your time in the same room as you speak, laugh, play music, and watch YouTube.

Texting and using Snapchat don't qualify as sending messages. If you meet together with your pals on a regular basis, you'll be happier and less worried. You want to get up close and personal with them, see their faces, gaze into their eyes, and enjoy typical adolescent activities. Sure, you are growing up and you are setting yourself up to be a mature and accomplished adult but you're still a kid and you should make sure you have time to act like one.

MEET WITH YOUR COUNSELOR

Although you'll be spending a lot of time with your buddies, you'll also be spending a lot of time with your school counselor too. Because they are the ones who are going to be helping you reach the next stage of your schooling career.

When you meet with your counselor during your junior year, you should ensure that your course schedule is on the right path and challenging enough to prepare you for the future beyond just college. If you are getting a good idea of the type of career you want to pursue, make sure that you discuss this with your counselor. They will tweak your schedule and classes in order to better equip and prepare you for the job of your dreams.

Your counselor will also help you prepare for any tests that you need to take, such as the SATs and ACTs. They will provide you with practice tests and walk you through what the entire process will be like.

Not enough people rely on their school counselors enough. They don't realize that they can provide you with the sort of tools that will set you up not only for university but for your career after that.

ATTEND COLLEGE & JOB FAIRS

At this point, you are starting to think about the jobs that will be right for you as you enter adulthood. And you will additionally also be thinking about which college will be a right fit for you. The two might go hand in hand. You might want to be a doctor or lawyer, which means that you will want to attend a law or medical school.

College and job fairs are going to be your friend when you are a junior and senior in high school. These will give you important information about both the schools and careers that are right for you. You will also make good connections there, with employers and experts in the chosen field that you're looking into.

Even if you're not entirely sure of which school or job that you want to pursue, you should still go to college and job fairs. You never know what sort of information will come your way at these events. There, you will get a good idea of your local area and the jobs that are out there waiting for you, relating to your dream job or not.

When you find a job or college that catches your eye, do your research about them. Look them up online, dig deeper into what they offer, imagine yourself pursuing them. That leads to the next thing that you should do when you're a junior in high school.

TOUR COLLEGE CAMPUSES

Whether it's near or far to your hometown, you might have a good idea of the college that you want to attend after you graduate from high school.

This is good news! It means that you're ahead of many people, especially if you have made this choice in your sophomore year, or early junior year. Many people wait much longer than that to settle down on the school that they want to attend.

But just because you have your eyes on a school doesn't mean your work is done yet. One of the smartest and best things that you can do as a high school junior is to actually attend the college of your choice. Obviously you won't be doing this as a student, but as a prospective one. This is done through college campus tours.

Nearly every single college offers tours for young people who are thinking of attending there. These are sometimes held on a regular schedule and sometimes have to be set up by you calling ahead and informing the school that you are thinking of dropping by and looking around. The tours will teach you a lot about the school, what it is known for, when it was founded, and more. And the tours will also show you around the campus, teach you where you will be studying, eating, and sleeping too.

In short, you should get a good feel for the college you're thinking of, for better or for worse. Some things that you witness will give you more reason to pursue the school in question. But some things might also detract from your interest and could make you second-guess your choice. All of this should be taken into account and weighed when you are making your final decision about the university that you'll be going to.

It is best if you schedule these tours with your family members, since they will likely be tied to your admission process and probably with paying for going to school too. That means that you might be spending part of your Thanksgiving, Christmas, or Spring Break going to these schools because that will likely work best for your parents' schedule.

LATE HIGH SCHOOL (11TH–12TH GRADE)

We are now rounding the corner and getting closer to the end of your time in high school. This means that we are also getting closer to your time in college, and your career. The picture is coming together, things are becoming more clear, and you are getting a better idea of what life after high school is going to look like, both in college and beyond.

The truth is that these last couple of years in high school will come with many tasks that you need to complete. That is because applying for and finding a college to call your own is honestly a lot of work. The process is long, complicated, and you have to do it the right way. And it doesn't start in the few months before you arrive for your first day of university. Instead, it actually starts a couple of years before. When you are a late junior and senior, much of your time will be dedicated to figuring out your college plans.

GET YOUR DOCUMENTS IN ORDER

One of the things that students don't think about when they are preparing for college, their careers, and the real world is that they need to prove to the world that they are real people. That might sound silly because, of course, you *are* a real person. But we all know that you need proof of that.

If you don't have it already, you need to obtain your social security number. You will definitely need this when you are applying for college and, after that, financial aid as well. Getting your social security number is a fairly easy process, as long as you have the right documentation. Your birth certificate will be needed, as well as some sort of state-issued ID too. Your parents will be able to help you with this part of the process, as they probably keep your birth certificate in a special, safe place.

Do you have a bank account? You definitely need one before you are starting to make your moves to college. Although you might not be paying for all of the things that you buy for your time in college (thanks, mom and dad!) you will still need to be spending a lot of money before and during your time at college.

PLAN FOR YOUR TESTS

We have made it clear that both the SATs and ACTs might not be as scary as some people make them out to be but they are still important and if you are applying for colleges then you should really schedule them into your 11th grade plans.

You should plan to take the ACT in February of your junior year, while you should be taking the SAT in March of the same year. You will want to touch in with your school counselor before you make any plans, as they will give you the study materials and practice tests that you will need.

If you have a university that you are fond of, you need to check their testing requirements. Some schools require different things and you could be making more work for yourself than necessary based upon the school that you are thinking of attending.

You should also make sure that you study before the tests, spending time in the weeks before each in the books, going through the study materials, and mentally preparing yourself for the task at hand. And you should also consider retaking the tests if you're happy with your score. Remember, not doing excellently on either of these tests isn't the end of the road for you, you'll still have plenty of great college options laid before you. But if you want to get a better score, for any reason, you should be prepared to take the tests again to truly show what you are capable of.

PREPARE FOR FINANCIAL AID

The sad truth is that college is incredibly expensive these days. Attending a school is far more expensive than it was only just a decade ago. That means that financial aid is more important than ever before.

While your parents might assist you a lot with how you pay for school, you'll still want to apply for financial aid. Anything to make your life - and your parents' life - easier is better.

Applying for financial aid takes a lot of work. But don't worry, you will have help. Many community colleges hold weekly nights where they help students get their paperwork in order and prepare them to apply for aid. You should check in with your school counselor and get advice on where to go and what to do when it comes to applying for and receiving your financial aid.

APPLICATION MATERIALS

Applying for college involves more than simply filling out a form and submitting your GPA from high school. You will also need letters of recommendations and essays when you are applying for college.

You should start to plan for both of these months before you are applying for your university. That is because the people who are writing your recommendation letters need as much advance notice as possible. If they are popular teachers of community members, there are probably multiple people asking them for this favor. That means they have a lot of writing to do and you want to go as easy on them as possible! As for your essay, you don't want to turn in a first draft. Instead, you want to put in as much work and energy as possible when you are compiling your essay. You also need to re-read, have others critique it, and perfect it so it is really the sort of essay you can be proud of and want to turn in.

CONCLUSION

High school is a lot of work - but it can also be a lot of fun too. You will be doing many things to lay the foundation for your college experience and career path when you are traveling through high school. There is so much work to be done, in fact, that you have to start thinking about it at the very beginning, when you are still a freshman in school.

From hanging out with friends, volunteering, getting advice, applying for college, and thinking of the career that awaits you, it might sometimes feel like there is *too* much to do when you are in high school. But the truth is that this is all very manageable, as long as you break it down year-by-year and stay on schedule and hold yourself accountable.

Each and every year in high school will be filled with fun and work. And when you combine both together, and don't neglect the other, you will find that you are setting yourself up for a wonderfully successful time after you graduate.

6 | POST HIGH SCHOOL PLAN

You did it. You earned your cap and gown, you walked in front of your friends and family and received your diploma. You graduated from high school.

That was a lot of work, but you should expect more now.

From college to what comes after, these are the years where you will be transforming into the young adult that you want to be.

While these next few years are going to be mostly about your college experience, you should also be well aware that this is when you will really start to plan for the dream job that will come after. Yes, there is a lot on the line and, yes, there is plenty of work to do. But you can do it all if you balance it well, plan accordingly, and stay hard at work.

The good news is that you have already proven you can do all of that. That's the biggest reason why you got through high school so easily, because you were taking it seriously, planning well, and sticking to the formula that worked best for you. So, in essence, your years in college and after high school will just be a continuation of that.

TWO—YEAR UNIVERSITIES

Some people bash on community colleges, also commonly called two-year universities, but they are actually incredibly helpful and useful, especially for young people who are on a budget. With the help of community colleges, millions of students have been able to live at home and save on transportation and living as well as other expenses.

Over the last generation, community colleges have exploded in popularity and have become far more efficient. Instead of the end of the road, they are now seen as a helpful stepping stone that will get you to the four-year university of your dreams. Admittance into a community college is far, far easier than getting into an established four-year university. And after spending two years in the community college of your choice, you are able to then transfer to the four-year school.

This means that because of the agreements between four-year and two-year schools, transfer students can earn their bachelor's degree while only spending two year's worth of higher tuition.

This process has helped so many people bypass extra expenses. During that time, you can also be working at a part time job, one that is in the field or industry that you want to pursue after graduating.

You should do some research of the community colleges around you. It is never too early to be studying subjects that will help you on your career path. Spend your time at a two-year university wisely and you will get the best out of it.

One of the other huge benefits of a community college is that it provides great flexibility in the schedule for students. Classes are held throughout the day, from morning to night, which will allow you to get a part time job.

This is particularly important for people who are trying to set out on the career paths they have envisioned. Via community college, you will be able to balance both education and working hard on the dream job that you want to have.

In sectors like medicine or police work, community colleges frequently offer a wide variety of career and technical education degrees. These courses help students become ready for the workforce.

Two-year colleges provide a wide range of professionalized education that four-year institutions sometimes do not, from mechanics to culinary arts. Although students might also study these subjects in a trade school, community colleges frequently offer these courses for much less money.

Millions of people pass up the chances that are offered to them by two-year universities because they aren't advertised as much. For generations, people have always assumed that the only way to go to college is with a four-year school. But that simply isn't true. Now is the time to seriously consider a two-year school if you are trying to get a good education, work hard at a job, and plan for a career after college.

WHAT ABOUT AN APPRENTICESHIP?

"An industry-driven, high-quality career pathway where employers can develop and prepare their future workforce, and individuals can obtain paid work experience, classroom instruction, mentorship, and a portable, nationally-recognized credential," is an apprenticeship, according to the federal government's definition.

Alternatively, to put it another way, an apprenticeship is a different approach to start a career in a certain industry.

For millions of people, earning an apprenticeship is a brilliant way to establish a strong future in any given industry. In fact, being an apprentice might even be better than going to college in some cases. This is especially true when you consider just how exorbitantly expensive going to college has become. Why should you spend all of that money when you can actually bypass school and still have a good - no, great - chance of getting the career of your dreams.

There are countless jobs that have apprenticeship programs. Some of them are more technical, such as plumbers and engineers and electricians. But there are other apprenticeships to less hands-on and intensive jobs, although they are not as common.

They are usually very appropriate for recently graduated high school students, but they might be advantageous for seasoned workers wishing to switch fields too. For instance, they could be helpful to a professional transferring to a new region where a formal certification is required.

But since you are a teen trying to make a life for yourself in a given profession that appeals to you, apprenticeships are extraordinarily perfect. Not only will you make money, but you'll get the sort of experience that will give you years and years in the industry that intrigues you.

That's right, you'll make money even though you are an apprentice. While they carry out their work responsibilities and gain knowledge from seasoned experts during the apprenticeship program, apprentices are actually paid a wage. This is a huge benefit, especially for young people who are used to unpaid internships. Now, the starting wage for an apprentice might not blow your hair back but rest assured that you'll always have room to grow and make more if you stick with it and continue to grow and thrive.

The experience that you receive while an apprentice is invaluable and can truly be the thing that grants you an entire career in the field of your choice. Think of it this way: even after spending three to four years in school, you might not have the abilities necessary to succeed in your chosen field of employment. And, more importantly, you may have never put your learned skills into practice. But when you become an apprentice, you gain practical work experience from a professional in your industry. It assists you in acquiring the skill set necessary for a selected vocation. For instance, you may gain practical experience using cutting-edge equipment while enrolled in an apprenticeship program.

Even if you don't stick with the company that you earned your apprenticeship with, you are still getting a leg up on many others and will surely find work in the industry elsewhere. That is because apprenticeships provide so much practical experience, companies frequently favor individuals who have completed them when they are taking on new employees for great wages.

A certificate of apprenticeship is a great method to demonstrate your worth to potential employers. It sets you apart from other applicants for the same position and tells companies that you have been trained by real professionals. You haven't just studied the profession in school but you have actually gotten out in the real world, "in the field" as they say, and have great experience.

Your company will pay you a salary or stipend each month during the apprenticeship. This enables you to pay your bills while finishing the academic and practical training. When you seek jobs in a certain sector, finishing such a program could boost your earning potential. For that and so many other reasons, getting an apprenticeship might be the right choice for you when you are setting forth on the career path that you have dreamt up. If the job you want allows for you, you should absolutely look into finding one.

TRADE SCHOOL

A trade school is a place where students may learn and receive hands-on training for a particular profession or vocation. These programs concentrate on the skills and education required within a particular sector, as opposed to requiring students to complete coursework that are unrelated to their job. Using this method, students get the competence and confidence they need to work in their desired industries.

While some trade courses might be short, some professions within a trade could need more knowledge or training. The duration of a trade program depends largely on the abilities and information required to send a student into the workforce with assurance.

By doing some exploration before selecting a certain school, you will discover which might be the right match for you. It might end up being much better and smarter than a four-year degree or starting your career path at a two-year university.

Whereas certain trade schools provide a more basic education in the trade, others may concentrate on a specific craft or vocation. To choose the program that will be the greatest match for you, it is a good idea to conduct some analysis on both trade institutions as well as the courses provided by them.

It's important to keep the program timeframe and tuition costs in mind while you research trade schools and their programs. This might help you assess whether attending a technical school is financially feasible for you and will also give you some idea of when you'll be able to begin your career path.

For some people, going to school and earning a degree is the best way to establish themselves for a long and fruitful career. However, some people don't have to do all of that. Depending on the job you are looking for, you can skip all of that and immediately get your foot in the door and burst onto the career path that you have created for yourself. A trade school will educate you just like a college does, but only about the specific things related to your future job.

FIND A JOB

If you are someone who knows exactly what career you want to pursue and know that you don't need formal training or certification to do so, you might be able to bypass all types of schooling in favor of just jumping directly into your job.

The moment that you graduate from high school can be the moment that you start applying for the job that you want. If you are able to and nothing is holding you back, why not?

Some careers require that you spend many years climbing a ladder, receiving promotions, and working your way to the top. If that's the case for your dream job, then you would be smart to start early, as soon as you can. Any time that you aren't working is time that you are wasting, in other words.

Before you follow through with this plan, it is downright vital that you ensure the job you're looking at doesn't require any sort of formal education if you aren't going to get one. But don't just think about the starting position that you'd get going with. Are there any positions higher up in the company that you'd like to possibly pursue someday? Do *they* require a degree of any type? If so, you need to plan ahead.

Finding a job right out of high school can be a great step that gives you the chance to get started on your dream career right away, without the waiting and the years spent in school. But it's only possible for certain jobs so you should be sure ahead of time and do the research needed.

GAP YEAR

Have you ever heard of a high graduate taking a "gap year" before they start college? It is fairly common, especially in European countries, and it could be right for you.

A gap year is when a student takes a year off from education and instead travels around the country or world, focuses solely on themselves, and enjoys some much-earned downtime with friends and family and by themselves.

It's quite an appealing idea, isn't it? Yes, it can come with many benefits. The biggest benefit is that you are able to focus on the things that you really enjoy instead of putting all of your time and energy into going to school.

If you plan for a gap year well ahead of time, you can even have a school or profession to come back to when your time traveling and relaxing is done. You can be accepted to a college that you'll start learning at a year *after* you graduate from college. Or you could have a career connection lined up so that you can slip right into a job when your gap year concludes.

The biggest problem with gap years is that they can be very tempting, in the worst ways. After twelve months of enjoying your life, you may not want to get back to the hard work of school or finding the job that is right for you. That is why you should only pursue a gap year if you have certain checks and balances in place to ensure that you won't turn a gap year into gap *years*.

7 | THINK OUTSIDE THE BOX

Your time in school is done and you are ready to burst out into the real, adult world and start down the career path you have put so much time and effort into.

For many people, that path looks exactly as they imagined. They have studied in school or an apprenticeship or trade school and they are ready to apply for jobs and finally use the experience they have to land one.

Others have bypassed school entirely and have spent the last few years getting experience and working hard and preparing to make an impression on the business or industry that they are drawn to.

But it is important to note that now, more than ever before, there are a variety of ways to find and pursue a career. Years ago, your parents were only able to find their job with one very specific and proven path. But today you have plenty of choices and options, depending on the dream job that you desire to have.

The truth is that you don't need to follow a traditional career path, like others before you have. You are not required to necessarily clock in at 9 AM and then clock out at 5 PM, like your parents and grand-parents before you did.

What has changed and how does the modern work landscape look?

FREELANCING

Over the last few years, freelance work has absolutely exploded in popularity and it's not more common to land this sort of job instead of a more traditional, old-fashioned type of profession.

What is freelancing and why might it appeal to you as a young person? Freelancing is simply a form of self-employment where you are typically paid by client, per project, per task, or per hour. Freelance workers often have several employers at one time and are usually doing multiple tasks at once.

Perhaps you are transcribing a podcast into a script. Maybe you are writing articles for an outlet on a semi-regular basis. Maybe you are doing bookkeeping or graphic design. It doesn't matter what the particular job is, freelancing is a way for you to work for multiple companies and do jobs here and there when they need you.

Freelancing isn't always steady but it does pay well. However, you have to keep in mind that you will be fighting against many competitors trying to land the same job. Therefore you must be able to really deliver on the promises you make, quickly and professionally. You should also have a pay quote that is going to impress your potential employers and make them even more enticed by your offerings.

The good news is that there are so many avenues for you to find freelancing jobs these days. Multiple websites allow you to make an account, apply for jobs, and interact directly with the employer offering jobs. It's all become so much easier than it ever was. There were times when temp agencies would help you find freelance jobs but now the power is in your hands.

From websites to message boards to simply posting on your Facebook, you can find a variety of freelance jobs today that just didn't exist even five years ago. The coronavirus pandemic made freelancing even more popular - and profitable. When everyone was stuck at home without a job, they turned to online freelancing to get by. And now the freelance market is more wild and inviting than ever before.

STARTING YOUR OWN BUSINESS

Along with freelancing, the internet has provided people with plenty more options to start their own businesses. From creating jewelry to making paintings to even more traditional tasks like data entry and accounting, it has never been easier to start your own business, either online or in person.

The use of social media and websites allows you to reach people like never before. Therefore, you can find a strong client base that is willing to pay you good money and give you a career, even if they live thousands of miles away.

If you want to branch out on your own and start your own business that is thriving, you need to go about it the right way. You need to be adamant about working hard and always getting better, as well as reaching out to customers, enhancing your skills, and dedicating a lot of time to your growing business.

No matter what this business of yours is, you cannot treat it like a hobby or just some side gig. Instead, you need to take pride and ownership of it and treat it like a true career, otherwise you will not dedicate enough energy to it. There are plenty of people who start businesses like this, advertise them a bit on social media, and then let them wither away and disappear. If you want to be better than them - and you do - you need to handle this as if it's a once-in-a-lifetime job opportunity that you cannot let pass you by.

You're a young person so chances are that you are quite talented when it comes to social media. You need to use that to your advantage if you are starting your own business. It's not enough to just post on your Facebook wall that you have a new company and want your friends to ask you about it. No, you need to create a specific page for your business, as well as its very own website, Twitter account, Instagram account, and more. Again, this has to be treated like a thriving, worthwhile business. Do what you must to have people forget that this is an enterprise you started. Give it the sort of professionalism and attention to detail that Fortune 500 companies do.

As you can imagine, this will take work and it will take time. But you can do it. Pay close attention to other companies that you respect, especially those with a strong social media presence and a smart marketing approach. Take notes of what you love about them and apply it to your business. Perhaps you can take business classes at your local community college for a cheap fee, they will teach you more about accounting and marketing and plenty of other aspects of running a company.

Check out books from your local library about running a company, read the business section of the newspaper, and take pointers from those who have found great success in their given industry. There are so many ways to live and breathe your passion for running your company.

Don't get sidetracked and do not just let this fall by the wayside. If you devote the time and energy, you will find success.

TALK TO ADULTS WHO YOU TRUST

Finally, you should reach out to the older people in your life who you admire and get their advice about finding a career that is right for you. Whether it be a company that you start on your own or an es-tablished business, you should turn to those you believe in and trust.

There are hopefully several people in your life who have a career that you admire. Perhaps it is a teacher at your school, your mother or father, or a family friend who has found success in their field of industry.

No matter who it is, write up a list of questions that you want to ask them and then pick their brains when they agree to sit down with you. Ask them how they got into their profession, what challenges were waiting for them, what they had to learn, the biggest advantages and disadvantages of it. Let them paint a very vivid and complete picture of their work life.

It doesn't matter how similar or different their job is from the one that you are hoping for, there will be many things that you should pay attention to. You will get insight into the type of things you want to feel, the ways that businesses can take advantage of you, and the pitfalls that wait for you if you don't look out for yourself and demand respect from your employer.

In short, ask this adult in your life how they got to the point they are at now, and leave them with one, major question: how do I become successful like you are?

CONCLUSION

Great things await you.

You are young, you are energetic and driven, and ready for the next steps in your life.

But the problem is that you might not be sure what those next steps are.

Today, now more than ever, there are so many job opportunities waiting for you. But these aren't just side gigs or small, part time jobs. Instead there are countless positions that can turn into full-time, long-lasting, successful and exciting careers. That is what you want. You are not looking for just something to pay the bills. Instead, you are looking for something that will make you excited to wake up every morning and head to work. You want something that will light a fire in you and make you passionate as well as financially healthy.

It's all out there waiting for you. You just have to know how to find it.

Firstly, you need to take your education seriously. It is not hyperbole to say that high school is very important and can set the tone and the foundation for the rest of your life. You need to attend your classes, study hard, and make sure that you give it your all.

That's because following high school is college and, for many people, college is the best way for you to find the career that is right for you. Via college, you will not only receive a degree but will learn many countless things about planning, critical thinking, working with others, communication, business, and more. And that degree or certificate that you receive from your university will go a long way with many industries and will get your foot in the door to a number of jobs. As much as times have changed, there are still plenty of companies that still want their employees to be college graduates.

But there isn't just college paving the way for your future career. Trade schools and apprenticeships could be the right path for you. They can give you hands-on training and intricate, detailed, vital education about the profession that you're chasing. What better thing to learn about your dream job than some serious experience?

Before you can do any of that, you need to think of the jobs that you want. You need to consider the professions that are successful and high-paying now and the ones that will stand the test of time and still be thriving in five, ten, and fifteen years beyond now. Some jobs have stood the test of time while others are only going to get more popular in the decades ahead. Consider these.

Consider the career clusters that we have told you about, as well. Spend time looking through each one and imagining yourself in each and every described field. Some might appeal to you, some won't. But you may be given an idea that you have never considered before. You never know when you might stumble upon a dream job that you never thought of.

Stay curious and stay fascinated by the growing and constantly-changing job landscape that exists.

The world is waiting for you and all the exciting opportunities and chances are all there, ready for you to take advantage of them. You just need the knowledge - and the drive - to capitalize on it all.

Your dreams are attainable, no matter what they are. The career that you have always wanted can be yours, if you do the work and the planning and take it seriously. You are at a very exciting moment in your life when so much is laid before you. You are about to step forward into adulthood and down the career path that can lead you to many wonderful, fruitful, memorable years. The time for you to start planning for that is now.